KEEP IT
SEASONAL

SOUPS, SALADS, AND SANDWICHES

KEEP IT
SEASONAL

ANNIE WAYTE

WITHDRAWN

WM

WILLIAM MORROW

An Imprint of HarperCollinsPublishers

PHOTOGRAPHS BY CHRISTOPHER GLASIER

HarperCollins books may be purchased for educational, business, or sales promotional use. For information please write: Special Markets Department, HarperCollins Publishers, 10 East 53rd Street, New York, NY 10022.

FIRST EDITION

Photograph styling by Marie Vadillo-Glasier

Designed by Leah Carlson-Stanisic

Printed on acid-free paper

Library of Congress Cataloging-in-Publication Data

Wayte, Annie.
Keep it seasonal: soups, salads and sandwiches / Annie Wayte – 1st edition
p. cm.
ISBN-13: 978-0-06-058392-7
ISBN-10: 0-06-058392-4
1. Cookery 2. Soups 3. Salads 4. Sandwiches I. Title.
TX714.W293 2006
641.5'64-dc22   2005050228

06 07 08 09 10 WBC /IM 10 9 8 7 6 5 4 3 2 1

CONTENTS

ACKNOWLEDGMENTS

A most important thank you goes to Christopher Glasier. His spectacular photography allowed me to realize my ambitions for *Keep It Seasonal*. He gave me the confidence to work without props, without cheating, and without strobe lighting! I thank him dearly for this. I shall always treasure our friendship.

A million thanks to my stylist, Marie Vadillo-Glasier. Her talent for bringing appeal and vibrancy to each picture is unquestionable. I can't thank her enough for the time she devoted to this project.

Thank you, Marie and Christopher, for traveling many eventful miles to shoot the dishes. Whether it was braving the freezing winter temperatures or enduring mosquito bites in soaring heat, you were both full of enthusiasm and support. For that I will always be grateful.

A special thank you goes to all the purveyors who generously contributed to the book, especially to the late Gary Feldman and to Joe Trapani, Mrs. Frances Smith, Charlie Andrews, Ted "Wildman" Dobson, Jan Greer, Michael Kokas, Frank Sorbello, Robin Lauriault, Yun Hinder and George, and Mrs. Kirkham. Without their passion for and dedication to providing fantastic products, cooking would not be nearly as inspiring or as joyous.

A big thanks to all my friends who helped along the way, especially to those who opened their homes to photo shoots—Curtis Gribble, David Diaz, Oscar Henquet, Nick Conlin, Noel Reghanti, Cedric Glasier, Stephen Brady, Sharon Bottom, and Laurent Hazan.

Thank you, Michael Mayhew, for your generous hospitality and for years of support, encouragement, and friendship.

Many thanks to the Nicole Farhi Home Collection for loaning many of the beautiful housewares that grace the photographs in the book.

A big thanks to Tina Bourbeau for her patience, help, and extraordinary creativity.

Thank you to all those who have helped further my culinary knowledge over the years, including past and present staffs—in particular Ed Witt, Florence Drean, and Benoit Boulanger.

Thanks to David Ramchal and The Color House.

Thank you, Ianthe Dugan and Dennis Berman for your invaluable editing assistance.

A special thank you to Stephen Marks, my boss and patron for the past decade, for his respect and trust. Were it not for his generosity, this book would never have been made.

Thank you, Michael Carlisle, for tasting my food and encouraging me to write this book.

Thank you, Harriet Bell, my editor, for trusting me to get on with it.

My parents, Michael Wayte and Elizabeth Simpson, deserve special thanks for supporting my passion.

Finally, this book could not have been completed without my husband and part-time guinea pig, Matthew. Thank you for eating, listening, and criticizing constructively. Most of all, thank you for your never-ending encouragement and for giving me the confidence to go for it!

INTRODUCTION

Working as the head chef at restaurants in London's swank Mayfair district and New York's Madison Avenue over the past decade, I have witnessed a growing trend among patrons. Customers who once opted to cut deals and schmooze over heavy four-course power lunches are increasingly choosing the soups, salads, and sandwiches on my menus.

There are several reasons for this shift. These smaller plates are great for busy people who do not want to be weighed down by heavier meals. They taste great. They also happen to be healthy.

As a result, I've put together a book on how to prepare soups, salads, and sandwiches as meals. While we might not all be busy with the latest corporate takeover, we do have families, friends, and jobs, and as a result, very little time for cooking. Meals at home ought to be relatively simple and quick to prepare. I, for one, like nothing more than a beautiful fresh salad and a glass of wine when I get home late from work.

Soups, salads, and sandwiches also are a great way to showcase fresh products. In fact, they force you to use top-notch ingredients. You can always mask a second-rate pork butt with a long, slow braise, but the simple preparations of soups, salads, and sandwiches demand fresh elements that taste great before they ever hit the chopping board.

To help you find ingredients every bit as good as those I use at the restaurants, I've organized the recipes seasonally. But what does "seasonal" mean exactly?

"When is apple season?" I recently posed this question to a smart acquaintance and was answered with a blank stare. Not even fifty years ago, everyone knew the answer. People were connected to the land through seasonal harvests that brought produce to their local market. Today we can run to the supermarket any time of year, in any part of the country, and grab a pint of strawberries (think summer) and a rutabaga (think winter doldrums) at the same time. All this choice has deadened our senses and opened the door to mediocre food.

Why buy asparagus out of season at sky-high prices? Or strawberries in winter, when they are watery and tasteless? They might

look good, but what's important is how they taste. Seasonal produce is more affordable, and its flavor and nutritional content are at their peak.

Since part of my job as a chef is to locate sources for ingredients, I know many of the people who grow the vegetables and fruits and raise the animals we use in my kitchens. I've threaded profiles of some of them through the book in hopes of spurring you to take a few more seconds each week—and perhaps a few more cents—to search out products being grown in your community. Visiting with these folks, I've learned how much time, work, and money it takes to grow a tomato and why paying a little extra for local products is worthwhile.

Buying locally grown produce is even more important than buying organic—another popular term. An "organic" label certifies that the grower avoided pesticides and didn't pretty up the produce with chemicals. Organic products are great and I support organic farmers as much as possible, but people often confuse organic with quality. The fact is that a tomato grown locally (especially in your backyard) is going to taste better than an organic tomato grown three thousand miles away.

The reason: modern transportation. Products must be picked unripe so that they will hold up better over the hundreds or thousands of miles of travel to our supermarket shelves. California strawberries eaten out of the field in the Central Valley are one of the earth's greatest pleasures. Those same berries bought in a New York supermarket could hardly be less exciting. If you buy unripe produce, no recipe is going to make it taste better. Premature picking aborts the process through which fruits and vegetables synthesize sunlight into the various chemicals that make food taste good.

Cooking out of season also cheats you of one of eating's greatest joys: the anticipation of that first sun-warmed tomato, freshly dug new potato, or crisp autumnal pear.

In each chapter here you will find a brief list of foods that reach maximum ripeness in that season. Use these as a guide to what

is available, but bear in mind that seasons are not always predictable and often overlap. (Heaven knows—I've spent years in England waiting for summer to arrive!) Obviously the same items are in season in different parts of the country, not to mention the world, at different times. For instance, springtime asparagus, baby lettuces, and strawberries are available earlier in California than in Pennsylvania.

Once top-quality ingredients are rounded up, some of the best ways to showcase them are in soups, salads, and sandwiches. You can prepare these in myriad ways. Start a meal with a bite-size smoked salmon club. Let a salad of grilled swordfish with spicy red lentils take center stage. Finish with a luscious strawberry-rhubarb soup with warm almond madeleines on the side. Who says soups, salads, and sandwiches aren't exciting?

Sandwiches are paradoxically the most beloved and the most neglected creations in the culinary world. Millions of sandwiches are slapped together every day. They are made at delis with canned tuna and big slabs of cold pressed meat. They are tossed into lunchboxes and wolfed down by schoolkids and construction workers and nibbled on in little triangles at a British high tea. Sandwiches are an ideal and much overlooked conduit for fundamental nourishment, yet they are rarely thought of as appropriate for real meals. In the recipes that follow, I challenge this notion with sandwiches that defy convention, whether it's a fig and ricotta panettone sandwich for dessert, a delicate asparagus and egg salad sandwich for tea, or a sweet pain perdu for breakfast.

Just remember that no matter what the dish may be, you want to stay focused on showing off those ingredients. Salads should smell fresh and vibrant, look colorful, and offer a variety of textures from crisp leaves to toasted nuts to crunchy vegetables. Be very picky when buying your greens. Avoid wilting leaves; look for strong, healthy ones. Trim the greens gently to avoid bruising their delicate leaves.

Dressings require the right balance of acidity—from citrus fruit or vinegar—to bring the components together with fresh, clean flavors. By tasting the dressing before tossing the salad, you will learn how much oil and vinegar pleases your palate.

As a chef, I understand that producing a decent dish takes time and effort. As a wife, I've come to appreciate the limits of those who have not spent their lives over a range, so I have gone out of my way to make the recipes in this book easy to follow and relatively quick. Where possible, I suggest alternative faster preparations.

Many of the soup recipes, for instance, allow you to fall back on reliable "municipal stock" (tap water) as a base. On the other hand, making a stock is easy: Simmer the trimmings from vegetables, meat, or fish in a saucepan with a pinch of salt. Twenty minutes later, you have the foundations of a soup.

I've also added optional touches to enhance and dress up certain dishes. A spoonful of buttermilk or a swirl of yogurt allows a bowl of soup to stand out. Serve an accompanying treat on the side, such as a ginger-laced cookie or a savory cheese and thyme muffin. Remember that not every embellishment works with every soup. The ingredients should complement the flavor, texture, and visual appeal of the soup. For instance, if herbs season the soup base, garnish it with an herb fritter or with a generous scoop of herb-infused yogurt or cream to add a fresh, bright taste.

In addition to buying local produce in season, a well-stocked pantry is the key to cooking efficiently. I am never without extra virgin olive oil, garlic, and lemons. I keep a range of spices and condiments on hand, along with jars of good-quality olives, anchovies, and capers. Fresh herbs make a huge difference in cooking. Wrapped in damp paper towels and stored in a sealed plastic bag in the refrigerator, they will stay fresh for up to a week. I can't live without my mortar and pestle, which I use to bash garlic, lemon zest, and herbs or spices for marinating fish, meat, or vegetables.

The final ingredient to cooking well is confidence. Keep your mind open. Relax and experiment. Learn to taste food. Is it salty, sweet, spicy, or sour? If you like something, make a mental note of the taste. But also remember that ingredents do not consistently taste the same every time you use them. Be flexible and adapt the recipes according to what's fresh and in season. While this is one of the most difficult aspects of cooking, it is the key to becoming a good cook.

SPRING

SOUPS

Spring Vegetable Broth with Parsley-Parmesan Relish

Fresh Pea Soup with Morels

Watercress Soup with Crème Fraîche

Thai Spinach Soup with Lemongrass, Coconut, and Ginger

Asparagus and Prosciutto Soup

Chilled Asparagus and Almond Soup

Chicken, Leek, Potato, and Mushroom Soup with Thyme Muffins

Strawberry-Rhubarb Soup with Almond Madeleines

SALADS

Spring Vegetable Platter with Aioli, Tarator,
and Warm Anchovy Bath

Wild Salmon, New Potato, and Asparagus Salad
with Sorrel Dressing

Crispy Prosciutto and Leek Salad with Mustard Dressing

Lamb Carpaccio with Feta, Olives, Lemon, and Mint

Seared Tuna and Asian Greens with Cucumber Relish

Warm Broccoli Salad with Shaved Parmesan and
Black Olive Dressing

SANDWICHES

Spicy Lamb Sandwich on Flat Bread with Pistachio Relish

Vanilla-Poached Rhubarb on Raisin-Nut Bread with Thick Yogurt

Goat Cheese, Beet, and Watercress Sandwich on Multigrain Bread

Buffalo Mozzarella, Prosciutto, and Fava Bean Ciabatta

Asparagus and Egg Salad Sandwich

Vitello Tonnato on Pugliese with Capers, Red Onions, and Arugula

Hallelujah! I'm thrilled when spring arrives to rescue me from celery roots, parsnips, and rutabagas. I love the comfort of these winter foods, but by April I've had my fill. I'm now ready to usher in the vast range of spring delights. Warmer weather cajoles more flavor and sweetness in everything from new potatoes, to spring lamb, to pink rhubarb. Look for wild salmon at your fish store and wait patiently until late spring for sweet strawberries. Asparagus abounds from mid-April through mid-June. It has a short season, so buy with abundance and prepare it in as many ways as possible. Treat yourself to the crème de la crème of all mushrooms: morels. Amid these recipes, I will introduce you to Yun Hinder, who forages the hills of England's Pembrokeshire, Wales, for wild foods. You will also meet Ted Dobson, whose pretty patch of land in Massachusetts produces pungently flavored organic microgreens and herbs.

HERE IS A LIST OF SEASONAL SPRING ITEMS:

Artichokes
Arugula
Asian greens
Asparagus
Baby leeks
Beets
Broccoli
Cabbage
Chive flowers
Early pink rhubarb
Fava beans
Garlic flowers
Lamb
Morels
Mustard leaves
Nasturtiums
Peas
Radishes
Ramps
Sorrel
Spinach
Spring garlic
Spring onions
Strawberries
Watercress
Wild salmon

SPRING VEGETABLE BROTH WITH
PARSLEY-PARMESAN RELISH

What makes this soup so special is that it treasures the trimmings that other soups might overlook. And it tastes sumptuous with any vegetable at any time of year. Use this recipe as a guide, altering the types and quantities of the vegetables to suit your taste. Just remember to cook the "hard" vegetables (carrots, celery, fennel, celery root, onions), which are going to take the longest, first. Then add the "softer" vegetables (asparagus, peas, fava beans, leeks). Be sure to swirl plenty of the Parsley-Parmesan Relish into the soup to marry all the flavors.

 Since the stock utilizes the trimmings, you'll want to prepare the vegetables for the soup, then cook the stock.

 You can use this method throughout the year, varying the vegetables according to the season. In the summer, for example, make room-temperature minestrone by adding peeled and seeded tomatoes, cooked shell beans, diced bacon, and tiny pasta shapes. In the winter, try pearl barley and sliced rutabaga, parsnip, celery root, and potato. Serve it with warm goat cheese on toast. SERVES 4

1 teaspoon fresh thyme leaves

1 teaspoon fresh rosemary leaves

1 clove garlic, green shoot removed, minced

Sea salt

1 tablespoon extra virgin olive oil

2 carrots, peeled (trimmings reserved for vegetable stock), thinly sliced

1 small red onion, halved and thinly sliced

2 stalks celery, thinly sliced (trimmings reserved for vegetable stock)

1 bulb fennel (outside layer removed and reserved for vegetable stock), quartered and thinly sliced

4 cups Vegetable Stock (page 6)

1 leek (white part only), thinly sliced

5 spears asparagus, trimmed (ends reserved for vegetable stock) and sliced diagonally into bite-size pieces

Good-size handful fresh peas, shelled (shells reserved for vegetable stock)

Good-size handful fresh fava beans, shelled

Freshly ground black pepper

1 recipe Parsley-Parmesan Relish (page 6)

Combine the thyme, rosemary, garlic, and a pinch of sea salt in a mortar, and pound with the pestle until the mixture forms a coarse paste. Stir in the olive oil.

Place a large pot over medium heat and add the rosemary-thyme paste. Gently sauté for a couple of minutes, allowing the aromas from the herbs to develop. Add the carrots, red onion, celery, and fennel. Gently sweat the vegetables, being careful not to brown them, until they start to release their juices, 8 to 10 minutes. If the pan gets too hot, lower the heat slightly and add a spoonful of the vegetable stock.

Add the leeks, asparagus, peas, and fava beans, and sauté for another 5 minutes. Add the vegetable stock, increase the heat, and bring to a boil. Then lower the heat and simmer until all the vegetables are tender, 10 to 15 minutes. Taste the broth for seasoning and add more salt if needed. Add pepper to taste.

Ladle the broth into warmed soup bowls and top each serving with a generous spoonful of Parsley-Parmesan Relish. Serve the remaining relish on the side.

VEGETABLE STOCK
MAKES APPROXIMATELY 2 QUARTS

Don't be put off by the long list of ingredients in this stock. There is no hard and fast rule as to what goes into a vegetable stock, but do keep in mind that the mix you choose will greatly affect the ultimate taste. The sweetness of carrots, for example, tempers the bitterness of dark green leek tops. Celery adds a wonderful base flavor to any stock, but be sure to balance both dark and light green stems. The lighter the color, the milder the flavor.

Always wash vegetables prior to slicing, or you'll wash away the juices locked inside.

I like to add a scrap of ham or slice of bacon if I happen to have some in the refrigerator.

9 cups water

2 carrots, coarsely chopped, plus trimmings from Spring Vegetable Broth

2 stalks celery, coarsely chopped, plus trimmings from Spring Vegetable Broth

1 onion, coarsely chopped

1 leek, white part only, sliced

Pea shells from Spring Vegetable Broth

Fennel trimmings from Spring Vegetable Broth

Asparagus trimmings from Spring Vegetable Broth

3 cloves garlic, crushed

Good pinch sea salt

4 black peppercorns, crushed

Small handful parsley sprigs

Small handful rosemary sprigs

Small handful thyme sprigs

2 bay leaves

1 slice bacon, optional

Put all the ingredients into a large pot and place it over a high heat. Bring to a boil and skim off any scum that forms on the surface. Lower the heat and simmer the stock for approximately 25 minutes.

Remove the pot from the heat and strain the liquid through a strainer, discarding the solids.

Reserve the stock until required. The stock will keep for 2 days refrigerated.

PARSLEY-PARMESAN RELISH
MAKES 1½ CUPS

¾ cup coarsely chopped fresh parsley leaves

¼ cup coarsely chopped fresh mint leaves

½ clove garlic, minced

¼ cup extra virgin olive oil

½ cup freshly grated Parmesan cheese

Sea salt and freshly ground black pepper to taste

Place all the ingredients in a bowl and stir well to combine.

FRESH PEA SOUP WITH MORELS

A mere handful of morels elevates an otherwise humdrum pea puree into a soup with swagger! These amazing springtime mushrooms have an unusual honeycomb surface and an earthy, woody flavor. Look for morels that are on the drier side, as a moist interior is a perfect habitat for unwanted guests.

If you are unable to find fresh morels, try shiitake mushrooms; their flavor will marry well with the sweet-tasting peas.

SERVES 4

4 cups shelled peas, pods reserved

½ cup trimmed and sliced fresh morel mushrooms (trimmings reserved)

1 tablespoon coarsely chopped fresh mint leaves, stems reserved

Splash extra virgin olive oil

1 medium onion, finely diced

½ clove garlic, minced

Sea salt and freshly ground black pepper

1 teaspoon sugar

1 tablespoon butter

1 shallot, finely diced

½ teaspoon fresh thyme leaves

4 teaspoons crème fraîche

Prepare the pea stock: Place the pea pods, mushroom trimmings, and mint stems in a saucepan. Cover with water and bring to a boil over high heat. Then immediately lower the heat and simmer for 25 minutes. Strain the liquid through a sieve or colander, discarding the pods and trimmings. Set the stock aside.

In a large, wide saucepan, warm the olive oil over medium heat. Add the onions and gently sauté until translucent, approximately 10 minutes. Add the garlic and peas, and sauté for a couple more minutes. Season with salt and pepper. Stir in the sugar. Then add 2 cups of the pea stock and simmer until the peas are tender, about 10 minutes for young peas, 20 to 30 minutes for large starchy peas. Taste the peas after 10 minutes to test for tenderness.

As soon as the peas are cooked, remove two thirds of the soup from the saucepan and puree it, in batches, in a blender or food processor until smooth. Return the puree to the pan and stir until well combined and heated through. Taste the soup, and adjust the seasoning with salt and pepper if necessary. Set the soup aside.

Heat the butter in a skillet over medium heat until it starts to sizzle. Add the morels, shallots, and thyme, and season generously with salt and pepper. Sauté until the morels are golden brown and tender, approximately 10 minutes.

Reheat the soup and stir in the chopped mint. Divide the soup among warmed bowls. Top with a spoonful of crème fraîche and a scattering of sautéed morels, and serve.

MORELS

HERE ARE SOME OTHER IDEAS FOR MOREL SEASON:

Morels on Toast
Sauté a handful of morels, a crushed garlic clove, and a teaspoon of chopped fresh thyme in a generous slug of olive oil. Add ¾ cup mushroom stock (mushroom trimmings, a couple of dried mushrooms, a garlic clove, and a cup of coarsely chopped vegetables, such as carrot, celery, and onion, simmered in water to cover for 25 minutes, then strained) and simmer until it has reduced by half. Melt a generous spoonful of crème fraîche into the mushroom sauce, season with salt and pepper, and pour over toast.

Morel and Asparagus Salad with Warm Goat Cheese
Drizzle olive oil over a bunch of asparagus spears and a handful of morels. Season with salt and pepper, then roast in a preheated 375°F oven for approximately 15 minutes. Toss the asparagus and morels with salad greens, such as arugula, watercress, or pea shoots, and arrange on plates. Warm rounds of creamy goat cheese in the oven and place one on top of each serving. Blend 1 teaspoon Dijon mustard with a smidgeon of crushed garlic and 1 tablespoon white wine vinegar. Whisk in 3 tablespoons extra virgin olive oil and season with salt and pepper. Drizzle over the salad.

Morels with Scrambled Eggs
Sauté a handful of morels and a finely diced shallot in a generous knob of butter, and season with salt and pepper. Whisk 2 to 3 eggs per person in a bowl, adding salt and pepper to taste. Melt 1 tablespoon butter in a skillet over medium heat and add the eggs. Slowly stir the eggs until they begin to set. When they are cooked to your taste, stir in a large spoonful of heavy cream. Pour onto a warm serving plate and scatter the morels over the top.

WATERCRESS SOUP WITH CRÈME FRAÎCHE

Watercress, with its tangy, peppery flavor, is in full swing in April and May. When purchasing watercress, make sure the leaves are dark green, fresh-looking, and not wilted.

You need to work fairly quickly when adding the watercress in this soup, as its fragile color can diminish rapidly. Have all the ingredients ready before you start cooking. If you are not going to serve the soup immediately, place the pan in a large container filled with ice to chill the soup as quickly as possible.

Serve this soup either hot or cold. SERVES 4 TO 6

2 tablespoons butter

1 leek (white part only), sliced

1 medium onion, coarsely chopped

Sea salt and freshly ground black
    pepper

6 ounces potatoes, such as Yukon
    Golds, coarsely chopped

5 cups Vegetable Stock (page 225)
    or water

3 bunches watercress, trimmed

Approximately ½ cup crème fraîche

Melt the butter in a large saucepan over medium heat. Add the leeks and onions and season to taste with the sea salt and pepper. Gently sweat the vegetables, being careful not to let them brown, for 6 to 7 minutes. Add the potatoes, stir, and then add the stock or water. Increase the heat and bring to a boil. Then lower the heat and simmer until the potatoes are tender, 15 to 20 minutes.

Increase the heat again and add the watercress, reserving a few sprigs for garnish. The quicker the watercress wilts, the better chance of retaining its nutritive value and color. As soon as it has wilted, remove the soup from the heat and puree it, in batches, in a blender. Then pass the soup, pressing on it with a spoon, through a medium-fine sieve into a clean saucepan or a metal container. (If you aren't serving it immediately, a metal container will cool the soup quickly, helping to maintain its vibrant green color.)

Reheat the soup over gentle heat; do not allow it to boil. Or chill the soup and serve it in chilled soup bowls.

Spoon a generous amount of crème fraîche on top of each serving and garnish with the reserved watercress sprigs.

THAI SPINACH SOUP WITH LEMONGRASS, COCONUT, AND GINGER

Great for entertaining, this easy-to-make Thai-influenced soup has a vivid green color coupled with exotic flavors. In the recipe I suggest that you garnish the soup with a scattering of cilantro leaves. If you wish to be more adventurous, garnish with finely shredded fresh ginger and toasted shavings of coconut.

Buy the freshest spinach available and make sure to wash it a couple of times, as grit will stubbornly cling to the leaves.

To continue the Asian theme, follow the soup with Seared Tuna and Asian Greens (page 36). SERVES 6 TO 8

1 tablespoon butter

1 leek (white part only), sliced

1 onion, coarsely chopped

3 cloves garlic, coarsely chopped

½ stalk lemongrass, coarsely chopped

2 Kaffir lime leaves, optional (see Note)

½ bunch cilantro, coarsely chopped, including stems

2 tablespoons chopped fresh ginger

1 hot chile pepper, such as a Thai chile, coarsely chopped

6 to 8 ounces potatoes, such as Yukon Golds, coarsely chopped

4 cups Vegetable Stock (page 225) or water

Sea salt

1½ pounds spinach, trimmed and thoroughly washed

1 cup unsweetened coconut milk

Small handful fresh cilantro leaves, for garnish

Melt the butter in a large saucepan over medium heat. Add the leeks, onions, garlic, lemongrass, lime leaves, cilantro, ginger, and chile. Gently sweat the vegetables, being careful not to let them brown, for approximately 5 minutes. Add the potatoes and the vegetable stock or water, and season with a pinch of sea salt. Bring the soup to a boil. Then reduce the heat and simmer until the potatoes are tender, approximately 25 minutes.

Increase the heat and add the spinach and another pinch of salt. Stir well to combine. Once the spinach has wilted (1 to 2 minutes), remove the soup from the heat and puree it, in batches, in a blender until smooth. Pass the soup through a medium-fine sieve into a clean saucepan, pressing on it with a spoon. Add the coconut milk and stir well.

If you are not serving it straightaway, chill the soup over a bowl of ice. This will help maintain the vivid color.

When ready to serve, reheat the soup if necessary. Taste and adjust the seasoning with salt and pepper if necessary. Garnish with a scattering of cilantro leaves and serve.

NOTE:

Kaffir lime leaves, a Southeast Asian herb, have a wonderful fragrance and add a distinctive and refreshing lime-lemongrass flavor to sauces, soups, and cocktails. They can be purchased at Asian supermarkets. They freeze well in a Ziploc bag and don't need to be defrosted before use.

ASPARAGUS AND PROSCIUTTO SOUP

This soup captures the essence of springtime. It takes advantage of the bounty of asparagus that comes with the season and pairs it with the rich, salty taste of prosciutto. For the prosciutto, buy the end of the ham, called the hock. It is the fattiest and most flavorful section. Keep the hock in the refrigerator and slice off chunks to flavor soups, stews, and stocks. The hock will keep, refrigerated, for 3 to 4 months. SERVES 4

2 pounds asparagus, peeled, trimmed (trimmings reserved), and coarsely chopped, plus tips from 8 additional spears

One 3- to 4-ounce chunk of prosciutto hock (see headnote)

2 tablespoons butter

1 large leek, white part only, coarsely chopped

1 small potato, coarsely chopped

Sea salt and freshly ground black pepper

3 slices prosciutto, cut into thin strips, for garnish

Place the asparagus trimmings and the chunk of prosciutto in a saucepan, add water to cover (about 6 cups), and bring to a boil. Then lower the heat and simmer for approximately 35 minutes. While it is cooking, remove any scum that forms on the surface.

Remove the pan from the heat and strain the stock through a sieve. Discard the trimmings and prosciutto. Set the stock aside.

Melt the butter in a saucepan over medium heat. Add the leeks and sauté gently until tender, 3 to 4 minutes.

Add the potatoes, sea salt and pepper to taste, and 5 cups of the reserved stock. Bring to a boil. Then lower the heat and simmer until the potatoes are tender, 15 to 20 minutes. Increase the heat, add the chopped asparagus, and cook until it is tender, approximately 5 minutes. Remove the pan from the heat and puree the soup, in batches, in a blender. Then pass it through a fine-mesh sieve into a saucepan.

In the meantime, boil the reserved asparagus tips in salted water for 2 minutes to blanch them. Drain and set aside.

Reheat the soup, being careful not to let it boil (this would diminish the flavor). Garnish with the strips of prosciutto and the reserved blanched asparagus tips, and serve.

CHILLED ASPARAGUS AND ALMOND SOUP

This soup can be made 24 hours ahead and stored in the refrigerator. Stir it well before serving.   SERVES 4

2 pounds asparagus, peeled, trimmed (trimmings reserved), and coarsely chopped, plus tips from 8 additional spears

Sea salt

¼ cup sliced almonds

2 tablespoons butter

1 large leek (white part only), sliced

½ clove garlic or 1 bulb spring garlic, trimmed

2 ounces blanched whole almonds

Freshly ground black pepper

1 cup heavy cream

1 teaspoon grated lemon zest

Squeeze of lemon juice

Preheat the oven to 375°F. Place four soup bowls in the refrigerator to chill.

Place the asparagus trimmings in a saucepan and add water to cover (about 5 cups). Add a pinch of sea salt to the water and bring to a boil. As soon as it starts boiling, lower the heat and simmer for 25 minutes. Remove the pan from the heat and strain the stock through a sieve. Discard the trimmings.

Meanwhile, place the sliced almonds on a baking sheet and toast in the oven until golden brown, approximately 5 minutes. Set aside to cool.

Melt the butter in a saucepan over medium heat. Add the leeks and garlic and sauté until the leeks are tender, 3 to 4 minutes. Add the blanched whole almonds and continue to sauté for 5 minutes. Season with salt and pepper, and add 4 cups of the reserved stock. Bring to a boil. Then lower the heat to a simmer and cook for 10 minutes.

Increase the heat, add the chopped asparagus, and cook until tender, approximately 5 minutes. Remove the pan from the heat and puree the soup, in batches, in a blender. Pass the puree through a fine-mesh sieve, discarding any solids. Allow the soup to cool, then place it in the refrigerator to chill.

Meanwhile, boil the reserved asparagus tips in salted water for 2 minutes. Drain and set aside.

To make the lemon cream, pour ½ cup plus 2 tablespoons of the heavy cream into a bowl and beat with a whisk until thick. Fold in the lemon zest and juice, and season to taste with salt and pepper. Keep refrigerated until required.

When ready to serve, stir the remaining heavy cream into the chilled soup until well combined. Pour the soup into the chilled bowls, and garnish each one with a spoonful of the lemon cream, a few asparagus tips, and a scattering of toasted sliced almonds.

CHICKEN, LEEK, POTATO, AND MUSHROOM SOUP WITH THYME MUFFINS

This satisfying and healthy soup is a one-bowl meal. It can be made a day in advance. The stock requires a whole chicken but the soup doesn't use all of the cooked meat, so store the remaining chicken in the refrigerator for a salad or sandwich.
SERVES 4

2 tablespoons butter

1 tablespoon extra virgin olive oil

¼ pound mushrooms, such as chanterelle, shiitake, or oyster, trimmed and sliced (trimmings reserved)

1 clove garlic, green shoot removed, minced

2 teaspoons fresh thyme leaves

1 large leek (white part only), sliced

1 small potato, such as Yukon Gold or fingerling, cut into bite-size pieces

Sea salt and freshly ground black pepper to taste

4 cups reserved chicken stock (see below)

1 cup reserved cooked chicken (see stock recipe)

Handful spinach leaves, washed and trimmed

1 recipe Thyme Muffins (page 20)

Melt the butter and olive oil in a large saucepan over medium-high heat. Add the sliced mushrooms and sauté until they have started to turn a golden brown, 5 minutes. Then add the garlic, thyme, and leeks. Continue to sauté gently until the leeks start to wilt, 3 to 4 minutes. Add the potatoes, season with sea salt and pepper, and cover with the chicken stock. Bring to a boil and then lower to a simmer. Cook until the potatoes start to collapse and thicken the broth, approximately 20 minutes.

Add the reserved chicken pieces and cook until warmed through. Just before serving, add the spinach leaves and stir gently until they wilt. Serve with warm Thyme Muffins.

CHICKEN STOCK   MAKES 1 QUART

One 2- to 2½-pound chicken, excess fat removed

1 leek (white part only), coarsely chopped

1 carrot, coarsely chopped

1 stalk celery, coarsely chopped

1 onion, coarsely chopped

3 cloves garlic, coarsely chopped

Mushroom trimmings from soup recipe, above

2 sprigs thyme

Pinch sea salt

Pinch freshly crushed black peppercorns

Combine all the ingredients in a deep pot and add water to cover. Bring to a boil and skim off any scum that forms on the surface. Then lower the heat and simmer gently until the chicken is cooked, 35 to 40 minutes. (To test if the chicken is done, prick the thickest part of the leg with a fork and watch the juice run out. It will run clear, not pink, if it is cooked.)

Remove the pot from the heat, carefully place the chicken on a plate, and set it aside to cool. Strain the stock through a fine-mesh sieve, discarding the solids. Place the strained stock in a clean saucepan and simmer over medium heat until it has reduced

by one half, about 60 minutes. (This will increase the chicken flavor of the stock.) Set it aside.

When the chicken has cooled down, remove and discard the skin. Remove the meat from the carcass and pull or slice it into bite-size pieces. Reserve 1 cup of the chicken meat for the soup and refrigerate the rest for another use.

THYME MUFFINS   MAKES 12 TO 15 MUFFINS

The muffin batter will hold for 2 days, covered and refrigerated, allowing you to bake these muffins when you need them.

1 cup all-purpose flour
½ cup finely ground whole-grain yellow cornmeal
¾ teaspoon baking powder
½ teaspoon baking soda
2 teaspoons fresh thyme leaves
½ teaspoon dry mustard
Small pinch cayenne pepper
11 tablespoons freshly grated Parmesan cheese
¼ teaspoon salt
1 large egg
1 teaspoon sugar
4 tablespoons (½ stick) butter, melted and cooled
⅓ cup sour cream or crème fraîche
¼ cup milk
¼ cup goat cheese

Preheat the oven to 400°F. Lightly grease 12 to 15 cups in muffin tins.

Combine the flour, cornmeal, baking powder, baking soda, thyme leaves, mustard, cayenne, 9 tablespoons of the Parmesan, and the salt in a medium bowl. Set aside.

Whisk the egg and sugar in a bowl until well combined and light-colored. Slowly add the melted butter, stirring well. Then whisk in the sour cream and milk until combined. Add this mixture to the dry ingredients, mixing gently with a rubber spatula until the batter is just combined and evenly moistened. Fold in the goat cheese, being careful not to overwork the batter. The goat cheese will stay in small clumps.

Divide the batter evenly among the muffin cups and sprinkle the remaining 2 tablespoons Parmesan over the top. Place in the oven and bake until the muffins are a light golden brown, approximately 18 minutes. (To test if they are cooked, insert a skewer; if it comes out clean they are ready.)

STRAWBERRY-RHUBARB SOUP
WITH ALMOND MADELEINES

Rhubarb and strawberries is a classic combination. A perfumed sweet strawberry combined with the sour taste of rhubarb creates a wonderfully fragrant marriage.

For the best results, make sure that the fruit you are using is ripe. Taste a strawberry before purchasing. Very often they are beautifully red on the outside but turn out to be hollow and bland-tasting. Look for strawberries that are firm, red to the center, juicy, and sweet. Unfortunately ripe strawberries are fairly perishable and may last only a couple of days in the refrigerator. Those that last too long probably have been picked unripe and then treated with chemicals to prevent spoilage. Be patient and wait for the local crop of strawberries. You will be justly rewarded. SERVES 6 TO 8

1 pound rhubarb, trimmed and coarsely chopped

Grated zest and juice of 1 orange

Grated zest and juice of 1 lemon

¼ cup light brown sugar

½ vanilla bean, split, seeds scraped out

1 whole clove

1 pound strawberries, hulled and sliced, reserving 6 to 8 whole strawberries for garnish

3 tablespoons confectioners' sugar

Grated zest and juice of 2 limes

4 generous tablespoons buttermilk

1 recipe Warm Almond Madeleines (page 22)

Combine the rhubarb, orange and lemon zests, and orange and lemon juices in a bowl. Add the brown sugar, scrapings from the vanilla bean plus the empty pod, and clove. Stir well and set aside to marinate for at least 2 hours or overnight.

Toss the sliced strawberries, confectioners' sugar, and lime zest and juice in another bowl. Macerate for at least 2 hours, stirring occasionally.

Preheat the oven to 350°F.

Give the rhubarb a stir and place it in a shallow 7-by-11-inch ovenproof dish. Cover with foil and bake for approximately 20 minutes, or until the rhubarb is tender. Remove from the oven and allow to cool. Remove the vanilla pod and whole clove. Set aside ½ cup of the baked rhubarb. Place the rest in a blender and puree until smooth.

Once the strawberries have started to release their juice, give them a good stir, place them in a blender, and puree until smooth.

Combine the two fruit purees in a mixing bowl and taste. Adjust the flavor with either sugar to sweeten or lime juice to sharpen. Chill the soup in the refrigerator for a couple of hours or overnight. At the same time, place four soup bowls in the refrigerator to chill.

Divide the soup among the chilled bowls. Garnish with the reserved rhubarb and whole strawberries. Swirl a spoonful of buttermilk over the soup and serve with Warm Almond Madeleines on the side.

WARM ALMOND MADELEINES

2 extra-large eggs, separated

1 tablespoon light brown sugar

¼ cup superfine sugar

1 teaspoon honey

Drop vanilla extract

Grated zest of 1 orange

⅓ cup ground almonds

⅓ cup all-purpose flour

Pinch salt

10 tablespoons butter, melted

Pinch sugar

Preheat the oven to 375°F. Grease madeleine molds with butter and dust them with flour. (If you don't have madeleine molds, use mini muffin tins.)

Using an electric mixer on medium speed, beat the egg yolks with the brown and superfine sugars, honey, vanilla, and orange zest until the mixture is pale and thick, approximately 5 minutes. Using a spatula, fold in the ground almonds, flour, and salt. Gradually pour the melted butter into the flour mixture, beating constantly. When combined, set aside.

In a clean mixing bowl, whisk the egg whites and sugar until they form soft peaks. Fold the whites into the batter.

Place the batter in the prepared molds and bake for 5 minutes, or until the madeleines are golden brown and springy to the touch. Turn them out on a wire cooling rack and serve while still warm.

OTHER IDEAS FOR THE STRAWBERRY-RHUBARB PUREE:

- *Spoon the puree over thick Greek yogurt and sprinkle with pistachio nuts for breakfast.*
- *Use the puree as a base or topping for ice cream.*
- *Make a fruit fool by folding whipped cream into the puree and serving it with ladyfingers.*

SPRING VEGETABLE PLATTER WITH AIOLI, TARATOR, AND WARM ANCHOVY BATH

To avoid boring vegetable platters, be sure to focus on color and flavor, preferably featuring locally grown selections. There is no need to go mad and buy ten different vegetables. Choose whatever is in peak condition, avoiding items that may look the part but are tasteless, such as those that have traveled halfway across the planet.

These dips really enhance the platter. You don't need to make three dips, but I suggest a minimum of two for variety. The three I have suggested are particular favorites of mine: Aioli is a garlic-flavored mayonnaise. Try to avoid using store-bought mayonnaise, as the flavor can't compare to homemade. If you can find fresh spring garlic, use it for its sweet flavor. Tarator is a Turkish sauce made with walnuts, garlic, and bread. It goes well with grilled meats, fish, and vegetables. The anchovy bath is salty, rich, and unctuous. Trust me—it will liven up any raw vegetable!

Allow a small handful of vegetables per guest. You can prepare the vegetables ahead of time, but make sure you cover them with a damp cloth and store them in the refrigerator until ready to serve. The three dips can be made a day in advance.

Baby carrots

Beans, such as dragon's tongue, romano, and/or yellow wax, trimmed

Cooked baby beets, various colors

Fava beans, shelled, boiled for 1 minute, then plunged into cold water and the outer layer of skin removed

Fennel, tough exterior trimmed and cut into small wedges

Cooked artichoke hearts

New potatoes, cooked in salted water until tender

Celery hearts, trimmed

Thin asparagus spears, trimmed and peeled

Free-range eggs, boiled for approximately 6 minutes, chilled, then peeled and cut in half

Red chicory or belgian endive leaves, trimmed

Arrange any combination of vegetables attractively on a large platter and serve with the following three dips.

AIOLI   MAKES 1 CUP

½ clove garlic or 1 bulb spring garlic

½ teaspoon sea salt

1 large egg yolk

½ cup extra virgin olive oil

¼ cup sunflower oil or grapeseed oil

Lemon juice

Pound the garlic with the sea salt in a mortar and pestle, or process for a few seconds in a food processor. Add the egg yolk and mix thoroughly until thick and gluey. Then slowly start to trickle the olive oil and sunflower oil into the mixture, drop by drop, beating vigorously until emulsified. If it becomes too thick, add a drop of the lemon juice and then continue to beat until all the oil has been added. Adjust the seasoning and consistency with salt, pepper, and lemon juice to taste.

TARATOR   MAKES 3/4 CUP

1 slice white bread, crusts removed

1 clove garlic

Pinch sea salt

½ cup walnuts or pine nuts, toasted

2 tablespoons lemon juice

Cayenne pepper

Place the slice of bread in a small bowl, add water to cover, and set aside to soak.

Mash the garlic, sea salt, and nuts in a mortar and pestle until smooth, or process in a food processor.

Squeeze the water from the bread and add the bread to the mortar (or processor) along with 1 tablespoon of the water. Work with the pestle (or process) until the sauce is smooth. Adjust the consistency by adding more water if you like. Stir in the lemon juice and sprinkle generously with cayenne pepper.

WARM ANCHOVY BATH   MAKES 1½ CUPS

The best anchovies for this recipe are the ones that come packed in sea salt. Rinse and fillet them with your fingers. However, if you are working on a tight schedule, use anchovies packed in olive oil; remove them from the can and scrape off any excess oil.

1 bulb spring garlic or 3 cloves garlic

¼ teaspoon sea salt

Pinch freshly ground black pepper

6 anchovy fillets

1 cup extra virgin olive oil

3 tablespoons butter

Generous splash red wine vinegar

Grated zest of 1 lemon

Pound the garlic, sea salt, and pepper in a mortar and pestle to form a paste. Add the anchovies and pound until coarsely mashed.

Warm the olive oil and butter in a saucepan over medium-low heat. Add the anchovy mixture, vinegar, and lemon zest. Simmer gently for 2 minutes, stirring with a whisk. Serve warm.

WILD SALMON, NEW POTATO, AND ASPARAGUS SALAD WITH SORREL DRESSING

I am a huge fan of wild salmon. Its firm pink flesh is a world apart from the fatty orange flesh of farmed salmon. On the downside, wild salmon is much more expensive than farmed and is available only between early March and the end of September. A less expensive alternative to wild salmon is sea trout. If you choose farmed salmon, look for salmon labeled "organic." Very often this will mean the fish has been kept in reasonably sized enclosures with strict control over types of feed and use of chemicals. SERVES 4

COURT BOUILLON

1 carrot, thinly sliced

1 stalk celery, thinly sliced

1 onion, thinly sliced

1 bulb fennel, thinly sliced, optional

Small handful white peppercorns, crushed

Small handful coriander seeds, crushed

Sea salt

1 sprig parsley

1 sprig thyme

1 bay leaf

Splash dry white wine

Juice of 1 lemon

SALAD

1 pound boneless salmon fillet, skin on

8 new potatoes

12 asparagus spears, trimmed, blanched in boiling salted water until tender

1 teaspoon coarsely chopped fresh chervil

1 teaspoon coarsely chopped fresh dill

1 teaspoon coarsely sliced fresh chives

Grated zest of 1 lemon

Prepare the court bouillon: Place the carrots, celery, onions, and fennel in a saucepan, and add the peppercorns, coriander seeds, sea salt, parsley, thyme, and bay leaf. Pour in the white wine and lemon juice. Cover with water (about 4 cups) and bring to a boil. Reduce the heat and simmer for 35 minutes.

Submerge the salmon in the court bouillon and barely simmer (to prevent the flesh from being damaged) until the center is still slightly underdone, approximately 8 minutes. (To check, use a small paring knife to part the flesh.)

Transfer the salmon to a plate and allow it to cool. Discard the court bouillon.

Gently boil the new potatoes in salted water until tender, 18 to 20 minutes. Drain the potatoes, cool them slightly, then cut them in half and place them in a bowl. Add the asparagus spears, chervil, dill, chives, lemon zest, olive oil, and sea salt and pepper to taste. Stir gently and allow to marinate for 30 minutes.

Layer the watercress, asparagus, and potatoes on serving plates. Using your hands, gently pry the salmon into large flakes and arrange them throughout the salad.

1 tablespoon extra virgin olive oil

Sea salt and freshly ground black
    pepper

2 bunches watercress, trimmed

DRESSING

¼ cup mayonnaise (page 223)

Juice of 1 lemon

1 tablespoon coarsely shredded sorrel

Prepare the dressing: Dilute the mayonnaise with enough of the lemon juice to reach a pouring consistency and stir in the shredded sorrel. Drizzle this dressing over each salad and serve.

ASPARAGUS

Local asparagus has a short season. To make the most of its brief appearance, try some of these ideas:

Steamed Asparagus with Warm Egg and Butter Sauce
Boil an egg for 10 minutes. Cool it under cold running water and peel off the shell. Grate the egg on the medium blade of a box grater. Melt 4 tablespoons butter in a saucepan, and add the grated egg, some chopped fresh parsley, and a squeeze of lemon juice. Season with sea salt and pepper, and pour over warm steamed asparagus.

Asparagus Tempura
Lightly beat 1 egg with 2 tablespoons ice water. Gently stir in 1/2 cup cake or tempura flour and a pinch of sea salt. The batter should be lumpy. Coat the asparagus spears in flour and then dip them into the batter. Deep-fry in vegetable oil at 360°F until golden brown and crisp, 3 to 4 minutes. Drain on paper towels, and season with sea salt and cayenne pepper. Serve immediately.

Asparagus Tart
Fill a 10-inch prebaked tart shell (page 222) with a generous handful of blanched asparagus spears, 5 or 6 roasted sliced shallots, and 1 tablespoon thyme leaves. In a mixing bowl, whisk together 1 1/2 cups heavy cream, 3 eggs, 1 tablespoon finely grated Parmesan cheese, and salt and pepper to taste. Pour this mixture into the tart shell. Casually nestle small clusters of fresh ricotta or goat cheese in the custard. Bake in a preheated 375°F oven for 30 minutes, or until the custard is set. Serve warm.

Shaved Asparagus and Mushroom Salad
Shave a trimmed bunch of asparagus with a vegetable peeler, forming long strips. Finely slice 2 or 3 ultrafresh cremini mushrooms or white button mushrooms, and place them in a bowl. Add the asparagus strips, a handful of Parmesan shavings, and salt and pepper to taste. Whisk 3 tablespoons olive oil and 1 tablespoon lemon juice together, and drizzle this dressing over the vegetables. Toss to mix thoroughly. Arrange the salad over arugula leaves on a platter and serve.

THE PLEASURES OF
WILD FOODS

wood sorrel

Spending time with **Yun Hinder** is like reliving the thrill of childhood treasure hunts. Accompanied by his wirehaired Jack Russell terrier, George, Yun scours the British Isles for uncommon wild foods, such as hairy bittercress, sea beet, pennywort, gorse flowers, sorrel, and scarlet elf cup mushrooms. He then carefully packages these delicacies and mails them to many of London's prestigious restaurants. I have known Yun for about ten years and have enjoyed many an adventure with him and George. One of my favorite finds is wild wood sorrel, a delicate, pretty herb that bears beautiful white flowers in the spring. Its citrus zing goes wonderfully with many other foods. I like to sprinkle it on top of grilled wild salmon and then simply drizzle the salmon with extra virgin olive oil.

Another favorite is common sorrel. It is not related to wood sorrel but rather is a member of the dock family and is often described as being lemony and sour. This sharpness is fragile and is damaged by the air when the sorrel is cut, so it is important to eat the leaves as soon as they are prepared. Try tossing them, roughly shredded, in a salad, or wilting them into a butter sauce for poached fish.

I have great childhood memories of hunting for blackberries, a venture that always sent me home with a bountiful bowl of juicy fruit—along with a black-stained mouth and hands. I learned then to vet the berries by searching out the youngest leaves and popping a sprig in my mouth. I was always amazed by the surprising taste of coconut that preceded the intense, quintessential blackberry flavor. Try using wild blackberries for sorbet, infusing the coarsely chopped leaves into the sugar syrup. Add some zip to your next cocktail by putting whole blackberry leaves into an ice tray, covering them with water, freezing, and then popping the cubes into a drink.

Alexanders (sometimes called wild celery)
Blackberries, fruit and leaves
Chives
Clover
Dandelion leaves
Fat hen (lamb's quarters)
Fennel
Gorse flowers
Ground elder
Hairy bittercress
Hawthorne leaves, fruit and flowers
Nettles
Pennywort
Primrose flowers
Sea beet
Sorrel
Violet flowers
Watercress
Wild garlic

CRISPY PROSCIUTTO AND LEEK SALAD
WITH MUSTARD DRESSING

For this salad, choose a selection of leaves that have a pungent bite to them: mustard leaves, bittercress, watercress, arugula, upland cress.

If you can't find baby leeks, small leeks will do. Also, at this time of the year, ramps (wild leeks) are in season and would be an excellent choice.

For an extra-rich addition, boil 4 eggs for 6 minutes. Peel and cut in half, allowing the yolk to ooze over the salad.

SERVES 4

12 baby leeks or 4 small leeks
   (white part only), trimmed

8 ramps, trimmed, optional

8 slices prosciutto

Grated zest of 1 lemon

¼ cup Dijon mustard

1 teaspoon dry mustard

1 tablespoon sugar

2 tablespoons white wine vinegar

⅓ cup olive oil

Sea salt and freshly ground black
   pepper

4 handfuls mixed greens, such as
   watercress, mustard, and arugula

Preheat the oven to 375°F.

Bring a saucepan of salted water to a boil, add the leeks, and boil until tender, approximately 5 minutes. (To test, pinch them with your fingers—quickly so as not to burn yourself. If they give a little to the pressure, they are tender.) Do the same for the ramps if you are using them. Drain and set aside.

Place the sliced prosciutto on a baking sheet, being careful not to overlap the slices (you may have to do this in batches). Place in the oven and bake until the prosciutto is golden brown and crisp, about 8 minutes. Remove the prosciutto from the oven and sprinkle with the lemon zest while it is still warm.

To prepare the dressing: Combine the mustards with the sugar and vinegar in a small bowl. Slowly whisk in the olive oil until thick and creamy.

To prepare the salad, season the leeks and ramps with sea salt and pepper and toss with a spoonful of the dressing. Layer the leeks and ramps, prosciutto, and greens on four salad plates. Drizzle each plate with an additional spoonful of dressing and serve.

LAMB CARPACCIO WITH FETA, OLIVES, LEMON, AND MINT

Carpaccio, an Italian dish, is traditionally made with thinly sliced raw beef and served with olive oil and shaved Parmesan. I have slightly altered this tradition by using lamb instead of beef and by adding a restrained amount of olives and feta. Spring lamb is perfect for this, as it is meltingly tender and subtly flavored. The addition of mint and lemon will lift your palate, adding a fresh and fragrant flavor.

This is a great starter for a dinner party. I like to make a large platter and place it in the center of the table, encouraging my guests to help themselves. SERVES 4

Large handful arugula leaves

Four 3-ounce pieces boneless lamb loin, trimmed and pounded very thin (see Note)

Extra virgin olive oil

Sea salt and freshly ground black pepper

4 ounces feta cheese, cut or crumbled into small pieces

Handful (approximately 20) small fresh mint leaves

Handful (approximately 20) black olives (Greek Kalamata or Spanish Arbequina), pitted

4 lemon wedges, for garnish

Arrange the arugula leaves on a serving platter. Gently peel the paper, if any, from the lamb and arrange the slices over the arugula. Drizzle the olive oil over the lamb. Season with sea salt and pepper, and scatter the feta, mint, and olives over the top. Place the lemon wedges alongside and serve.

NOTE:
Ask your butcher to pound the lamb into paper-thin slices. If this is not possible, take each piece of lamb and sandwich it between two sheets of plastic wrap or parchment paper. Using a meat pounder or a rolling pin, pound the lamb firmly and evenly until it is as thin as you can make it without ripping it.

If you are not serving this immediately, cover the meat well and place in the refrigerator. It will keep well for up to 12 hours; any longer, and the meat will lose its color and flavor.

SEARED TUNA AND ASIAN GREENS
WITH CUCUMBER RELISH

It is imperative that the tuna you use in this recipe be absolutely fresh and of the highest quality, as you are only going to sear the outside of the fish; the center will remain raw. If you are not a sushi fan, you can go ahead and cook the tuna all the way through, but I think it compromises the texture and flavor of the fish.

A variety of Asian greens are available throughout the year. However, they flourish during the cool-weather months, when their leaves are tender and young. In the hotter months, when their leaves become coarse from too much sun, I prefer to steam or sauté them. If you have a mandoline, use it to slice the vegetables for the relish. SERVES 4

TUNA

1 pound skinless center-cut tuna loin

Extra virgin olive oil

Sea salt and freshly ground black pepper

RELISH

½ cup rice vinegar

3 tablespoons sugar

1 teaspoon coriander seeds

1 teaspoon yellow mustard seeds

1 small red onion, thinly sliced

1 bulb fennel, trimmed and thinly sliced

½ cucumber, peeled and thinly sliced

4 pink or red radishes, sliced into thin rounds

4 fresh water chestnuts, peeled and thinly sliced, optional

¼ cup fresh cilantro leaves

¼ cup fresh mint leaves

Pinch cayenne pepper

Rub a drizzle of olive oil into both sides of the tuna, and season with sea salt and pepper. Heat a sauté pan over medium-high heat. Add the tuna and sear for 1 minute. Turn the fish over and repeat, searing the other side. Remove the tuna from the pan and set it aside to cool.

While the tuna is cooling, prepare the relish: Combine the rice vinegar, sugar, coriander seeds, and mustard seeds in a saucepan and bring to a boil. Reduce the heat and simmer until the mixture has the consistency of a thin syrup, 6 to 8 minutes. Remove the pan from the heat and allow the syrup to cool completely.

Combine the onions, fennel, cucumbers, radishes, and water chestnuts in a bowl. Toss with the cilantro, mint, and cayenne. Add just enough of the cooled syrup to coat the vegetables, and set the relish aside. (The remaining syrup will keep in a jar in the refrigerator for 1 month.)

DRESSING

¼ teaspoon minced hot chile pepper, such as bird's-eye or Thai

¼ teaspoon minced garlic

Grated zest and juice of 1 lime

1 teaspoon grated fresh ginger

¼ teaspoon Asian fish sauce

2½ tablespoons light soy sauce

1 tablespoon rice vinegar

¾ teaspoon toasted sesame oil

4 small handfuls Asian greens such as tatsoi, mizuna, baby bok choi, and cilantro shoots

To prepare the dressing, combine the chile, garlic, lime zest and juice, ginger, fish sauce, soy sauce, rice vinegar, and sesame oil in a small bowl and whisk to combine. Taste and adjust the seasoning, if necessary, with the various components.

To serve, gently toss the Asian greens with a spoonful of the dressing in a bowl. Divide them evenly among four plates. Slice the tuna into eight pieces and arrange them over the greens. Top with the cucumber relish. Finish each plate with a generous drizzle of the dressing and serve.

mizuna

MINIATURE GREENS

I must introduce you to **Ted Dobson**, a farmer in Massachusetts. It is Ted's contagious laughter, fueled by his passion for growing a wonderful array of microgreens, shoots, and herbs—from lemon basil bursting with citrus aromas, to a mesclun of unusual Asian greens, to a dainty ensemble of flower petals tossed with miniature arugula leaves—that imprints itself in my memory.

Ted's passion for the land encourages you to rethink how you purchase the food you eat. He encourages you to stop eating "foreign" food and look at what is grown locally.

In the mid-1980s Ted was at the cutting edge of his profession, introducing the consumer to intensely flavored, beautiful, and unusual mesclun greens. The integrity of these greens is a reflection of having been grown organically in the open air. Ted combines his mesclun greens with deliberation, ensuring that each mix sings with the correct balance of flavors. Baby arugula, red oak leaf, and mustard greens are finished with a sprinkling of red amaranth or salad burnet. A mix of baby Asian greens is tossed with micro cilantro shoots. Peppercress is left to speak for itself, with its fiery punch lingering on your tongue. These microgreens require little dressing—often merely a squeeze of lemon juice and a drizzle of olive oil.

Look for microgreens in your local farmers' market. Ask to taste them before purchasing, to see which flavors appeal to you. Get creative and blend your own mesclun. Experiment with the flavors, colors, and textures of the leaves by marrying them with meats, fish, and vegetables. For example, try a blend of baby red mustard leaves and peppercress with a roast duck and figs, or blend various kinds of shoots to give a crunchy texture to a piece of poached tuna.

LOOK FOR THE FOLLOWING SHOOTS AND MICRO-GREENS AT YOUR LOCAL FARMERS' MARKET:

Buckwheat shoots

Chickweed

Claytonia

Dandelion

Micro cilantro

Mizuna

Pea shoots

Purslane

Red mustard

Sunflower sprouts

Tatsoi

baby red mustard

microgreens

tatsoi

WARM BROCCOLI SALAD WITH SHAVED PARMESAN AND BLACK OLIVE DRESSING

Use any variety of broccoli for this recipe, from the mild standard broccoli to the stronger-flavored rapini, or broccoli rabe. When I am in England I can't wait to eat purple sprouting broccoli, which is available from mid-February through spring. Its tender stalk, leaf, and flower require little cooking, so it retains its high nutritional value.

Serve this as a side dish or as an appetizer. SERVES 4

1 teaspoon butter

2 tablespoons homemade toasted bread crumbs (see Note)

12 black peppercorns

1 clove garlic, green shoot removed, thinly sliced

2 tablespoons extra virgin olive oil

Sea salt

⅓ cup black olives, such as Kalamata or Niçoise, pitted

Squeeze lemon juice

½ pound broccoli, trimmed and cut into small branches

2 ounces Parmesan shavings (shaved with a vegetable peeler; about 8 large shavings)

Melt the butter in a sauté pan over medium heat, add the bread crumbs, and toast until crisp and golden, about 3 minutes. Set aside to cool.

Using the side of a wide-bladed knife, coarsely crush the peppercorns. Place them in a small sauté pan and toast over medium heat for 1 to 2 minutes, or until fragrant. Add the garlic and olive oil, and sauté gently until the garlic is slightly colored to a light gold, 1 to 2 minutes. Add a pinch of sea salt, the black olives, and the lemon juice. Simmer for a minute and then remove from the heat. Set aside to infuse for 15 minutes.

Just before serving time, bring a pot of salted water to a boil. Drop the broccoli into the boiling water and cook until tender, 3 to 5 minutes, depending on the thickness of the stems. Insert a small paring knife into the stems to test if they are tender.

Drain the broccoli and divide it among four plates, layering it with the Parmesan shavings. Warm the black olive dressing in a small saucepan over low heat and then spoon it over each plate. Finish with a generous scattering of the toasted bread crumbs and serve immediately.

NOTE:

To make toasted bread crumbs, remove the crust from 1 or more slices of stale bread and rip the bread into small pieces. Scatter the pieces on a baking sheet and toast in a preheated 375°F oven until dry, about 5 minutes. Remove the bread from the oven and allow it to cool. Then process the pieces in a blender or food processor to form crumbs. Stored in a resealable plastic bag in the freezer, these will keep for 1 month. (One slice of bread makes about ¼ cup crumbs.)

BROCCOLI

CHOOSING BROCCOLI:

Look for bright, fresh green florets. If the florets have started to turn yellow, the broccoli is past its best. This can often go undetected in plastic-wrapped broccoli in the supermarket because the discoloration usually hides on the underside of the florets. If you have opportunity to purchase broccoli from your local farmers' market, look at the different varieties available and if you are unfamiliar with them, quiz the farmer about their various flavors, which can vary from bitter to sweet to spicy.

SPICY LAMB SANDWICH ON FLAT BREAD
WITH PISTACHIO RELISH

People often associate the word "spicy" with "hot." This is not always the case. Many recipes use "warm" spices such as cumin, coriander, cardamom, nutmeg, cinnamon, and ginger. This lamb sandwich calls for a delicious—but not "hot"—Moroccan-style blend of spices.

As a quick alternative to the spice mix, simply squeeze fresh lemon juice over the lamb, add some crushed garlic, sea salt, and pepper, and allow it to marinate for a minimum of 1 hour. SERVES 4

SPICE MIX

3 teaspoons ground bay leaves

6 black peppercorns

4 teaspoons dried thyme leaves

1 teaspoon ground nutmeg

1 teaspoon ground cloves

1 teaspoon ground cinnamon

4 teaspoons ground coriander

1 teaspoon ground cardamom

2 teaspoons ground ginger

4 teaspoons ground cumin

1 teaspoon ground turmeric

1 teaspoon cayenne pepper

Sea salt

One 1¼- to 1½-pound piece boneless leg or shoulder of lamb (see Note)

One 12- to 14-ounce can chickpeas, drained

1 clove garlic

2 tablespoons lemon juice

1 tablespoon extra virgin olive oil

Pinch cayenne pepper

Sea salt

4 pita breads or other variety of pocket flat bread (see page 221)

4 small handfuls arugula

2 roasted red bell peppers, cut into large strips (see page 96)

1 recipe Pistachio Relish (page 43)

Prepare the spice mix: Grind the bay leaves and peppercorns together in a mortar and pestle or in a mini processor. Add all the remaining herbs and spices, including a generous pinch of sea salt, and mix thoroughly.

Pat a liberal coat of the spice mixture over the lamb. (Any remaining spice mix can be stored in an airtight container and used to season other meat and fish dishes.) Cover the lamb and set it aside to marinate for at least 2 hours at room temperature or in the refrigerator overnight. (If you refrigerate it, let it come back to room temperature before cooking it.)

Place the chickpeas and garlic in a food processor and pulse until the mixture forms a coarse mush. Add the lemon juice, olive oil, cayenne, and sea salt to taste. Continue to mix until it forms a fairly smooth puree. Set aside.

Preheat the oven to 390°F.

Place the lamb in a roasting pan and roast in the oven for approximately 35 minutes for medium doneness. If you prefer your meat well-done, leave it in the oven for another 10 to 15 minutes. Keep basting the meat with any fat that may have collected in the pan.

Remove the meat from the oven and let it rest for 5 to 10 minutes. Meanwhile, warm the pita in the oven for a minute or so. Then open the pocket of each pita and spread the chickpea puree inside. Slice the meat and stuff it inside the bread along with the arugula and the roasted peppers. Serve the Pistachio Relish alongside.

NOTE:

If you would rather cook the lamb on a barbecue grill or under the broiler, ask the butcher to butterfly it. (This means cutting the meat open to make a surface that is as even and flat as possible.) The cooking time will vary according to the thickness of the meat. As a rough guide, it will take a total of 5 to 6 minutes for medium-rare, 7 to 8 minutes for medium, and 10 to 12 minutes for well-done. Let the lamb rest for 5 to 10 minutes before slicing it.

PISTACHIO RELISH

Small handful unsalted pistachio nuts

Grated zest and juice of 1 lemon

Splash orange-flower water, optional

Smidgeon minced garlic

Small handful fresh flat-leaf parsley, coarsely chopped

Small handful fresh mint leaves, coarsely chopped

Extra virgin olive oil

Sea salt and freshly ground black pepper

Coarsely chop the pistachio nuts and place them in a medium-size bowl. Mix with the lemon zest and juice. Add the orange-flower water (often used in Moroccan cookery). Mix in the garlic, parsley, and mint. Stir in olive oil until the relish has a spreading consistency, and season with salt and pepper. Taste and adjust the seasoning if necessary.

ARTICHOKES

I LOVE TO SERVE THIS SANDWICH WITH A BOWL OF FRIED ARTICHOKES:
Peel off the tough outer leaves of baby artichokes and trim the stalks, leaving about 1 inch. Flatten each artichoke by turning it upside down and pressing down on it to encourage the leaves to open out like a flower. Season with sea salt and pepper.

Heat approximately 4 inches of vegetable oil in a deep-fryer or heavy pot to 350°F. Place a couple of artichokes in the oil and fry until golden brown and crisp, 3 to 4 minutes. Remove the artichokes and drain them well. Keep the cooked artichokes warm in a preheated 250°F oven while you fry the rest. Season them liberally with salt and pepper and serve with lemon wedges.

VANILLA-POACHED RHUBARB ON RAISIN-NUT BREAD WITH THICK YOGURT

Pale pink rhubarb first emerges in the very early spring. It is grown in covered "poly-tunnels," which keep the rhubarb warm, encouraging it to grow. As the season progresses into May, the field-grown crop of rhubarb appears in the market. Its characteristic tart and fruity flavor requires considerable sweetening.

Enjoy this sandwich for breakfast or dessert. It is particularly delicious on hazelnut-and-raisin bread, but other breads such as brioche or cinnamon-and-raisin would also be good. SERVES 4

½ pound rhubarb, trimmed, cut into ¼-inch-thick diagonal slices

Grated zest and juice of ½ orange

Grated zest and juice of ½ lemon

2 tablespoons light brown sugar

¼ vanilla bean, split open and seeds scraped

1 whole clove

1 tablespoon slivered blanched almonds

1 teaspoon confectioners' sugar, plus extra for dusting the sandwiches

4 slices raisin-nut bread

4 tablespoons thick Greek yogurt or thickened regular yogurt (see Note, page 97)

Combine the rhubarb, the orange zest and juice, and the lemon zest and juice in a bowl. Add the brown sugar, vanilla bean seeds and pod, and clove. Stir well, cover, and set aside to marinate for at least 2 hours or overnight.

Preheat the oven to 350°F.

Give the rhubarb mixture a stir and transfer it to a shallow ovenproof dish. Cover it with foil and bake for approximately 20 minutes, or until the rhubarb is tender when pierced with a knife. Remove the dish from the oven and let the rhubarb cool. The rhubarb will keep for 2 days, covered, in the refrigerator.

Preheat the broiler.

Place the almonds on a baking sheet and sift the confectioners' sugar evenly over them. Place under the broiler until golden brown, 2 to 3 minutes. Set the almonds aside.

Just before serving, toast the bread on both sides under the broiler. Place a slice of toast on each plate, and spoon a dollop of yogurt onto each piece of toast. Arrange the rhubarb over the top. Sprinkle with the toasted almonds. Dust the open sandwich with confectioners' sugar and serve while the toast is still warm.

GOAT CHEESE, BEET, AND WATERCRESS SANDWICH ON MULTIGRAIN BREAD

This is an excellent way to use leftover cooked beets. Or prepare beets according to this recipe and use them in a salad or as a vegetable accompaniment to a main dish. SERVES 4

2 bunches red and gold beets (approximately 12 beets), trimmed, skin left on

1 sprig thyme

2 cloves garlic, thinly sliced

1 tablespoon olive oil

Juice of 1 orange

Sea salt and freshly ground black pepper

8 slices multigrain or walnut bread

½ pound goat cheese, sliced

1 bunch watercress, trimmed

Preheat the oven to 375°F.

Place the beets in a baking dish and scatter the thyme, garlic, olive oil, orange juice, and sea salt over them. Cover the dish with foil and bake in the oven for approximately 40 minutes, or until the beets are tender when pierced with a knife or skewer.

Remove the dish from the oven and reserve the cooking juices. Set the beets aside to cool until you can handle them. Then peel the skin from the beets, using your hands (wear rubber gloves if you don't wish to discolor your hands), and slice them into thin rounds or wedges. Season the sliced beets with salt and pepper to taste, and pour the reserved cooking juices over them.

Preheat the broiler.

Toast the bread on both sides under the broiler. Add the sliced goat cheese to four of the slices and place them back under the broiler for 1 minute to warm and soften the cheese. Remove from the broiler and add the sliced beets and the watercress. Place the remaining toast on top, cut in half, and serve.

SPICY WALNUTS

I LIKE TO SERVE THIS SANDWICH WITH SPICY WALNUTS:
Place a generous shake each of cayenne pepper, chopped rosemary, paprika, ground cumin, sea salt, and ground ginger in a medium-size mixing bowl. Add a handful of walnut halves and a drizzle of olive oil. Stir well to coat the nuts evenly. Place on a baking sheet and roast in a preheated 375°F oven for approximately 10 minutes. The walnuts should release a wonderful aroma from the spices. Allow the nuts to cool; then store in an airtight container.

4 grape leaves (follow the instructions on the jar; they may need soaking prior to using)

4 teaspoons goat cheese

4 fresh sage leaves

Freshly ground black or pink peppercorns

Extra virgin olive oil

Lay the grape leaves, with the leaves pointing away from you, vein side up, on a work surface. Place a teaspoon of goat cheese close to the stem of each leaf. Lay a sage leaf on top of the cheese and season with pepper. Drizzle a little olive oil on top. Roll the leaf like a cigar, folding in the edges around the filling.

Warm a little olive oil in a sauté pan over medium heat. Gently fry the rolls until they are lightly browned and crisp all over, 5 minutes. Serve straightaway.

STEP ONE

STEP TWO

STEP THREE

BUFFALO MOZZARELLA, PROSCIUTTO, AND FAVA BEAN CIABATTA

Fava beans are the essence of springtime. They are wonderful served as a pureed soup, or cooked and whizzed into a garlicky dip, or marinated with other spring vegetables such as peas, asparagus, or artichokes. They go excellently in pasta or rice dishes. I have adapted this recipe from the Italian tradition of serving fava beans raw with small chunks of pecorino cheese to accompany an aperitif. In this case the fresh and zippy taste of the relish cuts through the richness of the prosciutto and seasons the mellow flavor of the mozzarella. Use young, tender fava beans. If they are hard and starchy, you will need to peel off their skins, which is a tedious job.

Try to buy imported mozzarella cheese from Italy for its soft and creamy texture. SERVES 4

6 ounces young fava beans, shelled

½ small clove garlic, sliced

Sea salt

12 fresh mint leaves

4 tablespoons freshly grated pecorino Romano or Parmesan cheese

1 tablespoon lemon juice

3 tablespoons extra virgin olive oil

Freshly ground black pepper

8 thin slices buffalo mozzarella

4 ciabatta or pugliese rolls

4 slices prosciutto

1 bunch arugula, trimmed

Preheat the broiler.

Place the fava beans, garlic, and sea salt to taste in a mortar and pestle and bash to form a rough paste. (If you don't have a mortar and pestle, pulse in a food processor.) Add the mint leaves and pound with the pestle. Stir in the pecorino, lemon juice, olive oil, and pepper to taste. Taste and adjust the seasoning if necessary by adding extra lemon juice, cheese, or salt and pepper.

Season the mozzarella rounds with salt and pepper. Slice each ciabatta roll in half and place the bottom pieces on a baking sheet. Place 2 slices of mozzarella on each bottom piece. Warm under the broiler just long enough to soften the cheese. Then remove the baking sheet from the broiler and place the cheese-covered rolls on four plates. Spoon the fava relish over the top, and add a slice of prosciutto and some arugula. Top with the ciabatta lids and serve.

ASPARAGUS AND EGG SALAD SANDWICH

This refined sandwich, with its delicate flavors and traditional white bread, is perfect to serve with afternoon tea. SERVES 4

3 large eggs

8 asparagus spears, trimmed

2 tablespoons mayonnaise (page 223)

Sea salt and freshly ground black pepper

8 slices white or brown bread

Small handful watercress, trimmed

Bring a small pot of water to a gentle boil. Add the eggs and boil for 10 minutes. Drain and plunge the eggs into a bowl of cold water to cool.

Meanwhile, fill a skillet with water and bring it to a boil. Add the asparagus and cook until tender, 3 to 5 minutes, depending on the thickness of the stalks. (If you have a steamer, it would be ideal for cooking the asparagus.) Drain and allow the asparagus to cool.

Place the mayonnaise in a large bowl. Peel the cooled eggs and chop them coarsely with a knife. Add the eggs to the mayonnaise. Slice the cooled asparagus into ½-inch pieces and fold them into the mayonnaise. Season with sea salt and pepper.

Spread one fourth of the egg-asparagus mayonnaise over a slice of bread. Add a layer of watercress and sandwich with another slice of bread. Use a bread knife to cut the crusts off the bread and then cut the sandwich in half diagonally. Repeat with the remaining bread and filling.

VITELLO TONNATO ON PUGLIESE WITH CAPERS, RED ONIONS, AND ARUGULA

This Italian classic gracefully mingles thin slices of poached veal, anchovies, capers, and a drizzling of tuna-based sauce. It sounds like a motley combination, but mixes surprisingly well and makes great fodder for a sandwich. SERVES 4

VEAL

1 carrot, coarsely chopped

1 stalk celery, coarsely chopped

1 onion, coarsely chopped

1 whole head garlic, cloves separated and coarsely chopped

1 sprig thyme

2 bay leaves

2 or 3 black peppercorns

Pinch sea salt

Generous splash dry white wine

1 pound boneless veal rump (this is from the top end of the leg)

SANDWICH

2 tablespoons canned Italian tuna packed in olive oil

3 anchovy fillets

1 large egg yolk

1 to 2 tablespoons lemon juice

¾ cup extra virgin olive oil

Sea salt and freshly ground black pepper

1 bunch arugula or watercress, trimmed

8 slices pugliese

2 teaspoons capers

½ red onion, thinly sliced

Poach the veal: Put the carrots, celery, onions, garlic, thyme, bay leaves, peppercorns, sea salt, and white wine in a large pot. Add water to cover and bring to a boil. Reduce the heat and simmer for 35 minutes. Add the veal and slowly bring back to a boil. Remove any scum that may appear on the surface. Lower the heat and simmer gently until the veal is tender, 20 to 25 minutes. The meat should be slightly pink in the middle. Be careful not to overcook it, or it will be dry and tough. Remove the veal from the pot and allow it to cool. Discard the solids, reserving the strained stock for future use in a soup or sauce.

Drain the tuna well and place it in a food processor. Add the anchovies, egg yolk, and lemon juice. Blend to form a paste. While the motor is running, slowly pour in the olive oil, emulsifying it into the tuna paste. Season the sauce with salt and pepper to taste. If the sauce is too thick to pour, add a little lemon juice or a splash of water to thin it.

Arrange some of the arugula on a piece of the bread. Slice the veal thinly and layer 2 to 3 pieces over the greens. Drizzle some of the tuna sauce over the veal, then scatter a few capers and red onion rings over the veal. Place a slice of bread on top. Repeat until all 4 sandwiches are made.

SUMMER

SOUPS

Chilled Melon, Ginger, and Mint Soup

Smoked Haddock Corn Chowder

Summer Squash Soup with Basil and Parmesan

Eggplant and Chickpea Soup with Chile Crème Fraîche

Chilled Red Pepper and Tomato Soup with
Cucumber-Herb Salad

"Peach Melba" Soup with Ginger-Pistachio Cookies

SALADS

Green Leaf Salad with Edible Flowers and Lemon Dressing

Swordfish, Spicy Red Lentil, and Zucchini Salad
with Yogurt Dressing

Tomato, Basil, and Ricotta Salad

Marinated Salmon and Fennel Salad with
Mustard-Dill Dressing

Shrimp and Cucumber Salad with Dill Crème Fraîche

Roasted Pepper, Eggplant, Cipolline, and Mozzarella Salad

SANDWICHES

B.L.T.

Moroccan Chicken on Coriander Flat Bread with
Carrot and Almond Salad

Tuna Ciabatta with Onion–Pine Nut Relish

Tuna Burgers with Avocado Relish

Warm Eggplant, Mozzarella, and Pesto Sandwich

Lemon Ice Cream Sandwich with Blueberry Compote

This is the time of the year to be laid back and let the ingredients speak for themselves. The supply of fruits, vegetables, and salad greens is abundant. Many of these are perfection eaten raw or cooked just briefly, marinated, and eaten at room temperature. A visit to a summertime farmers' market is a feast for the senses. Not only does the vast array of fruit and vegetables look stunning, but the sweet ripe melons, peaches, raspberries, and fragrant herbs contribute their intoxicating aromas to entice the shopper. Keep your recipe options open when you visit the market, allowing your culinary instincts to gravitate towards the best-smelling, -looking, and -tasting produce.

The summer welcomes us with the taste of succulent strawberries. Stone fruits, such as peaches, plums, nectarines, and apricots, follow close behind. By August, when eggplants, peppers, green beans, and zucchini abound, we know summer has truly arrived when we taste the first juicy, sweet tomatoes.

And best of all are heirloom tomatoes. They are bred for flavor, not for shipping. The seeds, handed down from generation to generation, yield soft-skinned, misshapen tomatoes in a variety of colors, oozing with sweet juices. They are the epitome of deliciousness and are showcased throughout this chapter.

ITEMS FOUND IN ABUNDANCE IN SUMMER:

Apricots
Beans
Berries
Carrots
Cherries
Corn
Cucumbers
Currants
Eggplants
Garlic
Gooseberries
Herbs
Melons
Nectarines
Peaches
Peas
Peppers
Plums
Potatoes
Radishes
Raspberries
Salmon
Shrimp
Summer squash
Swordfish
Tomatoes

CHILLED MELON, GINGER, AND MINT SOUP

This refreshing summer soup is quick and easy to make but requires juicy, perfectly ripe fruit. When selecting melons, smell them first: They should have a sweet fragrance. They should also be slightly soft at the tip when it is gently pressed. You can choose among a variety of melons: Try cantaloupe, honeydew, Crenshaw, Charentais, Galia, and Ogen.

I like this soup to have a bit of a ginger and chile kick to it, but by all means adjust the quantities to suit your palate. The yogurt, blended with the toasted coriander and pink peppercorns, acts as a soothing and fragrant partner to the soup.
SERVES 4

3 pounds ripe melon, peeled, seeded, and cut into chunks

3 tablespoons finely chopped fresh ginger

1 whole jalapeño pepper, seeded and finely chopped

1 teaspoon minced garlic

¼ cup coarsely chopped fresh mint leaves, plus 12 whole leaves, cut into strips

Grated zest of 1 lime

6 tablespoons lime juice (3 to 4 limes)

1½ teaspoons sea salt

1 teaspoon coriander seeds

1 teaspoon pink peppercorns

¼ cup yogurt

Place four serving bowls in the refrigerator to chill.

Combine the melon chunks, ginger, jalapeño, garlic, chopped mint, lime zest and juice, and salt in a blender and puree. Taste and adjust the seasoning if necessary: If you want the soup to have a healthy kick, add extra jalapeño or ginger. If the soup is too sweet, add extra lime juice. Place the soup in the refrigerator and chill for at least 4 hours.

Meanwhile, toast the coriander seeds and pink peppercorns in a small sauté pan over low heat for 2 to 3 minutes, or until fragrant. Allow to cool. Then, using the flat side of a chopping knife, crush the seeds and peppercorns. Place the yogurt in a small bowl and stir in the crushed spices. Set it aside in the refrigerator until ready to serve.

When ready to serve, divide the soup among the chilled bowls. Spoon some spiced yogurt over each serving and scatter the mint strips over the top.

SMOKED HADDOCK CORN CHOWDER

This chunky, rich soup, made with finnan haddock, potatoes, leeks, and milk, is an adaptation of the traditional Scottish soup called Cullen Skink.

Ask your purveyor where and how the fish is smoked. Request undyed smoked fish (you can tell the difference from the color of the flesh: If it is garishly colored, chances are it is chemically dyed). If you are unable to find smoked haddock, use smoked salmon or sturgeon.

Serve this chowder with warm crusty bread alongside. SERVES 4 AS AN APPETIZER OR 2 AS A MAIN COURSE

2 smoked haddock fillets, deboned

4 cups Vegetable Stock (page 225)

¾ pound small potatoes, such as fingerlings or Yukon Golds, sliced ¼ inch thick

2 tablespoons butter

2 leeks (white part only) sliced into ¼-inch-thick rounds

Kernels from 2 ears corn (see Note)

1 cup heavy cream

Sea salt and freshly ground black pepper

¼ cup chopped fresh flat-leaf parsley

Place the smoked haddock fillets side by side in a saucepan and cover with the vegetable stock. Bring to a boil and then remove from the heat. Allow the fillets to cool in the stock.

Once the haddock is cool enough to handle, peel off and discard the skin. Break the haddock flesh into chunky bite-size pieces and set aside. Strain the cooking liquid through a fine-mesh sieve, reserving 1 cup.

Place the potatoes in a small pot, cover with salted water, and bring to a boil. Cook until tender, approximately 10 minutes. Drain, discarding the cooking water.

To assemble the soup, heat the butter in a medium-size saucepan over medium heat. Add the leeks and sweat them until they start to soften (do not let them color), approximately 4 minutes. Add the reserved fish stock to the leeks and bring to a boil. After 2 minutes, lower the heat and add the cooked potatoes and the corn. Bring the soup back to a boil, and then add the cream and a pinch of sea salt and pepper. Simmer for a good 5 minutes, or until the soup has thickened slightly and is creamy; it should coat the back of a spoon. (The time can vary, depending on the fat content of the cream.)

Add the smoked haddock chunks and the chopped parsley and simmer for 1 minute, or until the haddock has warmed through. Taste, and add salt and pepper if needed. Serve immediately.

NOTE:
To remove the corn from the cob, stand the cob up on one end and run a knife down the sides, slicing off the kernels. Save the denuded cobs for making vegetable stock.

SUMMER SQUASH SOUP WITH BASIL AND PARMESAN

Farmers' markets carry summer squash in a wide range of colors, shapes, and sizes. Zucchini, crooknecks, and pattypans, to name a few, are immature fruits that lack abundant flavor. Due to their high water content (from just under to well over 90 percent), it is important to contrast the squash with stronger flavors or to cook them in a way that maximizes their taste. The majority of summer squash varieties take the same amount of time to cook, so they can easily be adapted to different recipes. This recipe calls for zucchini, but you can substitute others. Just make sure the squash is firm, with glossy skin; avoid scratched and blemished squash.

The combination of fresh mint, basil, and Parmesan infuses the zucchini with flavor. SERVES 4

2 tablespoons extra virgin olive oil, plus extra for drizzling

3 pounds zucchini, trimmed and cut into ½-inch dice

3 shallots, finely diced

1 clove garlic, minced

3 cups Vegetable Stock (page 225)

1 cup heavy cream

1 bunch fresh basil leaves, coarsely chopped

1 bunch fresh mint leaves, coarsely chopped

8 tablespoons freshly grated Parmesan cheese

Sea salt and freshly ground black pepper to taste

Heat the olive oil in a saucepan over medium heat. Add the zucchini and sauté until the squash is lightly colored, 12 to 15 minutes. Then add the shallots and garlic, and sauté for 5 more minutes.

Add the stock to the zucchini and bring to a boil. Reduce the heat and simmer for 5 minutes. Remove the pan from the heat.

Transfer approximately two thirds of the soup to a blender or food processor and puree. Return the puree to the remaining soup in the pan and set it over low heat. Add the cream and reheat the soup, stirring continually to prevent the soup from burning. Stir in the basil, mint, and Parmesan until well combined. Taste and adjust the seasoning if necessary.

Pour the soup into individual bowls and finish with a generous drizzle of extra virgin olive oil. Serve immediately.

SQUASH BLOSSOMS

Be on the lookout for squash blossoms during the summer months. Stuff their cavities with any of the following suggestions, then dip them in beer batter (see page 224) and deep-fry in vegetable or olive oil until golden brown and crisp. Serve as an accompaniment to the zucchini soup or as an appetizer on their own.

- *Small wedge of buffalo mozzarella wrapped inside a basil leaf*
- *Ricotta cheese mixed with slivers of prosciutto and chopped sage*
- *Goat cheese blended with chopped green olives, minced garlic, chopped fresh parsley, and grated orange zest*

EGGPLANT AND CHICKPEA SOUP
WITH CHILE CRÈME FRAÎCHE

Eggplants are available throughout most of the year, but they are at their best in the summer when they are sweet and carry fewer bitter-tasting seeds. There are many types available, from large, round, and black, to elongated varieties in multiple shades of purple, to small, white egg shapes. They range in taste from mild to bitter. For this recipe I suggest you use the standard large, round black variety.

When purchasing dried chickpeas, look for the packaging date, which will give you some indication of their age. Search for young chickpeas or "new season's" chickpeas. These will be tender and will therefore not take so much time to cook and, more important, will cook more evenly.

Note that dried chickpeas need to be soaked overnight. For convenience you could use canned chickpeas, but you won't get the valuable cooking liquid that can be used to make the soup; instead, substitute vegetable stock or water.   SERVES 6

2 cups dried chickpeas

2 eggplants (approximately 1¾ pounds total)

1 whole hot chile pepper, such as a Thai chile, plus ½ teaspoon chopped

8 cloves garlic: 6 crushed, 2 minced

1 bunch cilantro, leaves coarsely chopped, stems reserved

Sea salt

3 tablespoons extra virgin olive oil

1 cup diced shallots

2 teaspoons ground cumin

2 teaspoons ground coriander

½ teaspoon ground turmeric

½ teaspoon smoked paprika

2 tablespoons finely chopped preserved lemon

4 to 5 tablespoons lemon juice

(continued)

Place the dried chickpeas in a bowl, cover with water, and soak overnight in the refrigerator.

The next day, preheat the oven to 375°F.

Prick the eggplants with a fork (this prevents them from exploding while they're baking) and place them in a baking dish. Bake until the flesh is soft and tender, approximately 40 minutes. Remove the eggplants from the oven and allow them to cool. Then peel off and discard the skin. Chop the eggplant flesh until it resembles a coarse puree. Set it aside.

While the eggplants are baking, cook the chickpeas: Drain the chickpeas and place them in a large saucepan (the more room they have in the pan, the more evenly they will cook). Cover them with cold water and bring to a boil. Skim off any scum that appears on the surface and lower the heat to a gentle simmer. Add the whole chile pepper, crushed garlic, and cilantro stems. Simmer, stirring occasionally, for 25 minutes. Then add sea salt to taste and continue to simmer until the chickpeas are tender, approximately 25 minutes more. Remove the pan from the heat and set it aside to cool slightly. Then drain, reserving the chickpeas and the cooking liquid separately. Discard the chile, garlic, and cilantro stems. (If you are using canned chickpeas, simply drain them, rinse them under cold water, and proceed with the recipe.)

Warm the olive oil in a wide saucepan over low heat. Add the shallots, minced garlic, chopped chile, cumin, coriander, turmeric, and paprika. Sauté gently until the shallots are tender and translucent and the spices have released their wonderful fragrance, approximately 5 minutes. (If the pan gets too hot and the shallots look as though they may brown, add a splash of chickpea cooking liquid.)

Add the chopped preserved lemon, the eggplant puree, and the chickpeas. Season well with sea salt. Stir in 6 cups of the chickpea cooking liquid and simmer gently for 10

GARNISH

6 teaspoons crème fraîche

1 hot red chile pepper, such as a Thai chile, seeded and sliced into thin strips

¼ cup fresh cilantro leaves

¼ cup fresh mint leaves

1 tablespoon thinly sliced preserved lemon peel

minutes. Then transfer one third of the soup to a blender and puree. Return the puree to the saucepan, stirring well to prevent the soup from spitting. Stir in the chopped cilantro leaves and the lemon juice. Taste and adjust the seasoning if necessary.

Spoon the soup into individual bowls and top each serving with a dollop of crème fraîche. Scatter the chile strips, cilantro and mint leaves, and preserved lemon strips over the soup, and serve immediately.

NOTE:

This soup will keep well in the refrigerator for 2 days. When you reheat it, add a splash of water or stock, as the soup will have thickened.

PRESERVED LEMONS

Preserved lemons are used in Moroccan cookery. You can purchase them in jars at most supermarkets, but it is very simple to make your own: Wash several lemons. Using a paring knife, slit the peel vertically at several intervals around each lemon, cutting into the flesh of the fruit. Rub sea salt into each slit. Then place the lemons in a sterile jar, packing them tightly. Fill the jar with lemon juice, seal, and refrigerate. Allow the lemons to mature for at least 4 weeks before using them.

CHILLED RED PEPPER AND TOMATO SOUP
WITH CUCUMBER-HERB SALAD

I love the smell and look of this when it comes out of the oven—roasted tomatoes and peppers bubbling in a bath of olive oil, onions, and garlic. It is the deep roasting that brings out the sweetness of the tomatoes and peppers. Choose over-ripe tomatoes, as they will be extra-juicy. There is no additional liquid or stock in this recipe; the soup relies solely upon the juices extracted from the tomatoes and peppers, which culminate in an intense and concentrated flavor.

Serve it as a "salad-soup" similar in style to an Andalusian gazpacho: Half fill each bowl with soup; then pile a generous amount of cucumber salad on top. This makes for a satisfying lunch on a hot summer day. You may want to throw a few ice cubes into the soup to help maintain its chilled temperature. SERVES 4

SOUP

⅓ cup extra virgin olive oil

4 cloves garlic, crushed

1 hot red chile pepper, such as Thai or red jalapeño, halved

½ bunch cilantro

1 large onion, coarsely chopped

½ bulb fennel, coarsely chopped

3 red bell peppers, seeded and coarsely chopped

2½ pounds ripe tomatoes, coarsely chopped

2 teaspoons sea salt

Preheat the oven to 375°F. Place four soup bowls in the refrigerator to chill.

Combine the olive oil, garlic, chile pepper, and cilantro in an ovenproof pot and sauté over medium heat until the garlic is golden brown, approximately 5 minutes. Add the onions and fennel and sauté for 10 minutes. Then add the bell peppers, tomatoes, and salt. Stir well and transfer the pot to the oven. Bake, uncovered, stirring every 10 minutes or so, for 30 minutes, or until the contents have collapsed into their own liquid and appear scorched on top.

Remove the soup from the oven and allow it to cool for 20 minutes.

Ladle the soup, in batches, into a blender or food processor and puree until smooth. Then pass the puree through a sieve into a bowl, using a spoon to push as much through as possible. Discard the solids and refrigerate the soup for at least 3 hours.

SALAD

¼ English (hothouse) cucumber, peeled

¼ pound cherry tomatoes or small heirloom tomatoes (in a variety of colors if possible)

½ red bell pepper, seeded

½ yellow bell pepper, seeded

Small handful fresh basil leaves

Small handful fresh mint leaves

Small handful fresh cilantro leaves

Sea salt and freshly ground black pepper

GARNISH

Extra virgin olive oil

Prepare the salad: Cut the cucumber in half lengthwise and scrape out seeds with a teaspoon. Cut the cucumber halves into ½-inch diagonal slices and place them in a mixing bowl. Cut the cherry tomatoes in half and add them to the cucumbers. (If using heirloom tomatoes, cut them into small bite-size wedges.) Cut the bell peppers into attractive shapes, such as diamonds or thin strips. Add these to the mixing bowl along with the basil, mint, and cilantro. Toss with sea salt and pepper to taste.

Fill each soup bowl halfway with soup. Then arrange a generous amount of cucumber-herb salad on top. Finish with a drizzle of olive oil and serve.

"PEACH MELBA" SOUP WITH GINGER-PISTACHIO COOKIES

I was inspired to create this recipe after a trip to see Joe Trapani at Keepsake Farm in the Hudson Valley. On my return to New York City, I opened the car trunk to find, to my surprise, a bushel of his beautiful peaches. After making a dozen jars of peach jam, I wanted to move on to something new and decided to reinterpret a classic dessert, Peach Melba, turning it into a fruit soup.

Traditional Peach Melba consists of a layer of vanilla ice cream topped with peeled peaches that have been steeped in vanilla syrup, with a sauce of raspberry puree. For my soup version, I poach the peaches in a sugar syrup made with Prosecco, an Italian sparkling wine, and botrytis Sémillon, an Australian dessert wine. You could use any other type of dessert wine, such as a Sauternes or Muscat. The peaches are pureed, the vanilla ice cream placed in the center of the soup, and then the raspberry puree poured over the top. You can make all of the components a day in advance and then assemble the dessert shortly before serving it. The ice cream recipe makes 3 pints; you'll need only half that amount for 4 servings. In a pinch, use top-quality store-bought vanilla bean ice cream instead of making your own. SERVES 4

PEACH SOUP

2 cups Prosecco

¾ cup sweet dessert wine (see headnote)

2 cups sugar

2 cups water

2 pounds ripe peaches

2 tablespoons lemon juice

RASPBERRY PUREE

¾ pound fresh raspberries, hulled

¼ cup confectioners' sugar

1 tablespoon lemon juice

VANILLA ICE CREAM

2 cups half-and-half or milk

1 vanilla bean

10 large egg yolks

1 cup superfine sugar

3½ cups heavy cream

8 to 12 Ginger-Pistachio Cookies (page 76)

PREPARE THE PEACH SOUP:

Combine the Prosecco, dessert wine, sugar, and water in a saucepan, and stir over medium heat until the sugar has dissolved. Add the peaches and submerge them in the liquid, placing a small lid or plate on top of them to hold them down. Simmer gently until they are tender, approximately 20 minutes.

Using a slotted spoon, remove the peaches from the poaching liquid. Let them cool. Peel the peaches and remove their pits. Set 1 peach aside for the garnish. Place the remaining peaches, in batches, in a blender along with the lemon juice and approximately ½ cup of the poaching liquid. Puree until smooth. Then pass the puree through a sieve into a bowl and set it aside. If the puree is too thick for a soup, add more poaching liquid. (The remaining poaching liquid, stored in a sealed container in the refrigerator, will keep for at least 1 month. Use it to poach other fruits or to sweeten a cocktail.)

PREPARE THE RASPBERRY PUREE:

Place the raspberries, confectioners' sugar, and lemon juice in a blender and puree until smooth. Pass through a fine-mesh sieve into a bowl and refrigerate until ready to use.

PREPARE THE ICE CREAM:

Place the half-and-half or milk in a heavy-bottomed saucepan. Split the vanilla bean in half lengthwise and scrape the seeds out with a small knife. Add the pod and the seeds to the pan, set it over medium heat, and bring to just below the boiling point. Then remove the pan from the heat and set it aside to cool to lukewarm. When it has cooled, remove the vanilla pod.

Beat the egg yolks and the superfine sugar in a mixing bowl until well combined. Slowly pour the lukewarm vanilla cream into the egg mixture, whisking constantly so the eggs do not curdle. Return the mixture to the saucepan, and stirring slowly and constantly, heat it over medium-low heat until it starts to thicken and form a custard that will coat the back of the spoon, 8 to 10 minutes. Be careful not to let the custard boil. Remove the pan from the heat and pass the custard through a strainer into a bowl. Stir in the heavy cream and allow the mixture to cool completely.

Churn the ice cream in an ice cream maker according to the manufacturer's instructions. Then transfer it to an airtight container and place it in the freezer until frozen.

TO ASSEMBLE THE DESSERT:

Place four soup bowls in the refrigerator (or briefly in the freezer) to chill. Cut the reserved peach into thin slices.

Divide the peach soup among the chilled soup bowls. Place a scoop of vanilla ice cream in the center of each one and pour the raspberry puree over the top. Garnish with the peach slices and serve with the Ginger-Pistachio Cookies.

GINGER-PISTACHIO COOKIES   MAKES 24 COOKIES

2 large egg whites

Pinch sea salt

½ cup superfine sugar

½ cup all-purpose flour, sifted

4 tablespoons (½ stick) butter, melted and cooled to room temperature

Grated zest of 1 lemon

½ teaspoon ground ginger

¼ cup unsalted pistachio nuts, coarsely chopped

Preheat the oven to 375°F. Lightly grease two baking sheets with butter or grapeseed oil and line them with parchment paper.

Combine the egg whites, sea salt, and superfine sugar in a mixing bowl and, using an electric mixer, whisk until foamy, 2 to 3 minutes. Fold in the flour, butter, lemon zest, ginger, and pistachios until well combined.

Drop tablespoonfuls of the dough onto the prepared baking sheets, leaving a 3-inch gap between them. Using a palette knife or a small spatula, spread each cookie out to form a very thin round about 3 inches in diameter. Bake until lightly browned, about 5 minutes.

Wait for 15 seconds after the cookies come out of the oven. Then carefully lift each cookie up with a spatula and drape it over a rolling pin. As they cool, they will set and harden in that shape. (If they cool down too much and crack when you are draping them over the rolling pin, pop them back in the oven for a few seconds to soften and then proceed as before.)

Continue baking batches of the cookies, each time on a cool baking sheet, as described.

GREEN LEAF SALAD WITH EDIBLE FLOWERS AND LEMON DRESSING

This simple salad offers a chance to experiment with the many different varieties of greens available. The best way to discover which ones you like is to taste and decide whether you like bitter-flavored leaves such as endive or dandelion, or peppery leaves such as arugula or watercress, or a milder flavor such as oak-leaf or romaine lettuce. I suggest that you do not buy the ready-mixed bags in the supermarket unless they are from a reliable source, as very often they are sprayed with gases to extend their shelf life. SERVES 4

4 handfuls salad greens, such as arugula, red oak-leaf, and mizuna

Lemon Dressing (see below)

Selection of edible flowers (see page 81), for garnish

Just before serving, toss the leaves in a bowl with enough of the dressing to coat them. Arrange the salad on individual plates and decorate with the edible flowers.

LEMON DRESSING   MAKES ½ CUP

3 tablespoons lemon juice

¼ teaspoon Dijon mustard

5 tablespoons extra virgin olive oil

1 tablespoon chive buds

Sea salt and freshly ground black pepper

Combine the lemon juice and mustard in a small mixing bowl, and whisk in the olive oil. Add the chive buds, and season with salt and pepper to taste. The pretty purple blossoms of chives add a hint of onion flavor. Look for them at a farmers' market or, better yet, grow them in a small pot on your windowsill.

EDIBLE FLOWERS

pansies

For centuries cooks have acknowledged that edible flowers enhance the taste of food. Fortunately for us, as fashion dictates the trends, the culinary use of flowers is back in vogue. Some consider them too pretty to eat, but I believe they add an interesting taste as well as elevating a dish visually. If you are unfamiliar with edible flowers, begin by using them sparingly, incorporating them into dishes with other ingredients, as they can sometimes have an overpowering flavor.

Edible flowers can be purchased at gourmet markets, but I suggest you pick wildflowers or homegrown flowers; just remember to wash them before use. Remember that if a plant is edible, then so are its flowers. If you do not recognize a flower, you must determine its identity before you eat it. Have fun experimenting with the various colors of the flower petals, contrasting them with other elements on the plate.

If you are using herbs as part of a recipe, garnish the dish with their flower buds. For example, if you are making Chicken, Leek, Potato, and Mushroom Soup with Thyme Muffins (see page 18), scatter the thyme flowers over the soup. If you have chive or garlic flowers, use their pretty pink, mauve, and white petals to garnish soups or salads. Lavender buds crushed with sugar offer a fragrant flavor to ice cream or shortbread cookies (see page 113). Chopped nasturtium blossoms added to butter and then melted over grilled fish will add not only color but also a mild peppery spice. Once you have discovered the realm of cooking with flowers, there is no end to the possibilities.

Apple blossoms
Borage blossoms
Carnations
Cherry blossoms
Chive blossoms
Clover
Daisies
Dandelion blossoms
Dill blossoms
Hawthorne blossoms
Hibiscus blossoms
Lavender blossoms
Lovage blossoms
Marjoram blossoms
Nasturtiums
Pansies
Primroses
Roses
Scented geraniums
Violets
Zucchini blossoms

FLOWERS FOR
LUNCH

It was **Frances Smith** at Park Hill Farm in the small village of Appledore, in Kent, England, who first introduced me to edible flowers during a most notable luncheon.

Frances is a walking botanical encyclopedia, and having lunch with her is no ordinary experience. Upon my arrival she marched me up to her madly overgrown greenhouse, armed with a porcelain bowl to collect our lunch. On entering the greenhouse, I was greeted with intense, sweet herbal aromas: Texas wild tomatoes in one corner, pretty light green mizuna leaves in another, an array of unusual cane fruit, masses of multicolored nasturtium blossoms. The overriding winner for me was the enormous bright red dahlia buds. Mrs. Smith quite proudly announced that she had kept this plant since she was sixteen. (I don't think she will mind me saying that that would make the plant at least forty years old!) The buds looked primed to be judged for a horticultural show. Quite quickly I learned that this was to be the basis for our luncheon: these magnificent dahlia petals tossed with an assortment of home-grown salad greens and dressed in a vinaigrette of olive oil, a squeeze of lemon juice, a smidgeon of garlic, and freshly ground salt and pepper. The salad was simple and yet so delicious. The flecks of red petals not only looked stunning but also added texture and a mild peppery flavor.

So, next time you are presented with a dish garnished with flowers, don't be tempted to push them aside. Taste and decide for yourself if they are indeed too pretty to eat.

nasturtiums

SWORDFISH, SPICY RED LENTIL, AND
ZUCCHINI SALAD WITH YOGURT DRESSING

This summer salad, with its blend of warm spices, lemon, mint, and yogurt, is ideal for entertaining because most of the preparation is done in advance. Serve it as a main course, as it is quite substantial, and follow with the "Peach Melba" Soup with Ginger-Pistachio Cookies (see page 75). SERVES 4

SWORDFISH

Grated zest of 1 lemon

Smidgeon minced garlic

1 tablespoon olive oil

1 teaspoon chopped fresh marjoram
or mint

Eight 3-ounce swordfish steaks

8 strips lemon peel, including the pith,
blanched in boiling water for 30
seconds

8 fresh bay leaves

SALAD

¾ pound red lentils, rinsed

2 hot chile peppers, such as Thai
chiles: 1 whole, 1 chopped

2 cloves garlic, plus 1 teaspoon
minced garlic

Handful cilantro stems, plus handful
coarsely chopped cilantro leaves

Sea salt

3½ cups water

2 shallots, thinly sliced

Juice of 2 large lemons

½ cup extra virgin olive oil

½ bunch mint leaves, coarsely
chopped

Grated zest of 1 lemon

1 teaspoon ground cumin

1 teaspoon ground fenugreek

Freshly ground black pepper

Prepare the swordfish: Combine the lemon zest, garlic, olive oil, and marjoram in a mixing bowl. Add the swordfish and turn to coat the pieces with the mixture. Thread 2 pieces of swordfish, alternating with the lemon peel and bay leaves, on each of four metal skewers. (If you are using wooden skewers, soak them in water for 20 minutes before using.) Set the skewers in a large baking dish, cover, and marinate in the refrigerator for about 2 hours.

Place the lentils in a saucepan and add the whole chile, whole garlic cloves, cilantro stems, and 2 teaspoons sea salt. Add the water and bring to a boil over high heat. Then reduce the heat and simmer gently until the lentils are tender, 10 to 20 minutes, depending on the variety and age of the lentils. (To test, remove a few lentils with a slotted spoon and taste them. They should be tender, neither hard nor mushy.) Drain the lentils and discard the chile-garlic, and cilantro stems. Let the lentils cool to room temperature. The marinated lentils can be made without the fresh herbs a day in advance and stored, covered, in the refrigerator. Remove the lentils from the refrigerator at least 1 hour before continuing with the recipe and serving.

Combine the shallots and the juice of 1 lemon in a large bowl, and set aside to macerate for at least 20 minutes. Then add the chopped chile, minced garlic, chopped cilantro leaves, and a generous slug of the olive oil. Stir in half the mint leaves along with the lemon zest, cumin, and fenugreek. Add the lentils, stir well, and taste. Adjust the seasoning with any of these components. (I enjoy this salad quite spicy hot, so I tend to be generous with the chile and garlic.) Gently toss the arugula with the lentils.

Using a vegetable peeler, peel the zucchini into ribbons. When you get to the center of the zucchini, where the seeds start to appear, stop peeling and discard that part. Place the ribbons in a bowl, and just before serving, mix with a small splash of the remaining lemon juice and olive oil. Toss in the remaining mint, and season with sea salt and pepper.

Prepare a hot grill or preheat the broiler. Place the swordfish skewers on the grill or under the broiler, and cook for approximately 2 minutes on each side, depending on the thickness of the fish. (I like the fish to be juicy in the middle, so I slightly undercook it. To test the fish, press your thumb on the flesh. If it is medium, it will have a slight spring to the touch. If it is well-done, it will be firm to the touch.)

1 bunch arugula leaves, trimmed

2 zucchini

1 recipe Yogurt Dressing (see below)

While the swordfish is cooking, spoon the lentils onto dinner plates. Then arrange the swordfish skewers over the lentils, and scatter the zucchini on top. Serve the Yogurt Dressing on the side.

YOGURT DRESSING   MAKES 1/4 CUP

1/4 cup yogurt

1/4 teaspoon ground cumin

1/4 teaspoon ground ferugreek

Smidgeon minced garlic

Juice of 1 lime

Sea salt and freshly ground black pepper to taste

Combine all the ingredients in a small bowl and mix well. Taste and adjust the seasoning as necessary. This will keep for 24 hours, covered, in the refrigerator.

FISH

HELPFUL TIPS ON FISH:

Make sure you purchase the freshest fish possible. The skin should look shiny and healthy; the eyes should look bright and alert, not sunken; and it should not smell strong and fishy. Poke the fish: it should be resilient to the touch. And it should feel wet and clean, not sticky or slimy. Look for wet, reddish pink gills.

Ask your fishmonger to prepare the fish for you if it needs to be filleted, deboned, or skinned. This takes the hard work out of the preparation, so when you get home, you can concentrate on cooking it.

Finally, be careful not to overcook fish. Fish fillets cook in 4 to 5 minutes, making them ideal when you are on a tight schedule. Whole fish—poached, grilled, or fried—requires a little more skill and time, but it's well worth it. The natural flavor from the bones permeates the flesh, making it that much tastier.

OLD-FASHIONED
FLAVOR

Husband and wife team **Jan Greer** and **Mike Kokas** are the owners of Upstate Farms, in the Hudson Valley. Theirs was one of the first farms in New York State to produce heirloom tomatoes. Over the years they have produced more than seventy varieties.

Spending time with Jan and Mike helps you appreciate why farming is not for the faint-hearted. Through their passion for organic produce, they want to re-educate people about food. It sounds simple, but their business is under threat from large commercial farms. Most people aren't selective about what they eat. It's all about pricing. Forget seasonality. Forget flavor.

The seeds of heirloom tomatoes were handed down from generation to generation because the tomatoes tasted so wonderful. Commercially grown tomatoes, on the other hand, are bred for increased yield and ease of shipping. They are cheaper. They also have less flavor.

The next time you are in a supermarket, sample a tomato. How does it taste? What is its aroma? Then compare that to an heirloom tomato at your local farmers' market, and you'll see why Jan and Mike emphasize the merits of buying local and seasonal, and keeping it simple.

Amish Paste
Aunt Ruby's
Black Prince
Brandywine
Cavern
Federle
German Green
German Stripe
Gold Medal
Red Zebra
Soldacki
Stump of the World
Watermelon Beefsteak
Yellow Taxi

Heirloom tomatoes are prized not only for their various shapes, sizes, and colors, but for their outstanding flavor.

TOMATO, BASIL, AND RICOTTA SALAD

The simplicity of this salad highlights the true taste of the tomato. The other ingredients are there to bask in the glory and to soak up the luxurious tomato juices.

If you are able to find different varieties of tomatoes, showcase their individuality by slicing and arranging them to complement their unique shape and color. Look for the many varieties of heirlooms.

Choose a ricotta that is moist, sweet, and smooth. If you can purchase ricotta from an Italian delicatessen where they make it on the premises, all the better. SERVES 4

2½ pounds heirloom tomatoes in various shapes, sizes, and colors

½ clove garlic, plus ¼ teaspoon minced garlic

½ hot chile pepper, such as Thai

2 tablespoons lemon juice

4 tablespoons extra virgin olive oil

Sea salt and freshly ground black pepper

One 3-ounce chunk day-old country-style bread

3 tablespoons finely diced red onion

Small handful fresh basil leaves

½ cup ricotta

Coarsely chop approximately ½ pound of the tomatoes. Place them in a blender and add the half clove of garlic, chili pepper, lemon juice, 2 tablespoons of the olive oil, and a good pinch of sea salt and black pepper. Puree the mixture. Then pass the puree through a sieve into a bowl, pressing on the solids with a spoon. Discard the solids. You should end up with approximately 1 cup of tomato juice.

Remove the crusts from the bread and rip it into roughly shaped croutons. Place them in a bowl and toss with half of the tomato juice. Set aside to soak.

Meanwhile, slice the remaining tomatoes in various shapes and sizes, according to your preference, and place them in a medium-size bowl. Season with sea salt and black pepper. Add the red onions, the minced garlic, and the remaining 2 tablespoons olive oil. Mix well and set aside to macerate for at least 30 minutes, stirring every so often.

When you are ready to serve the salad, gently toss the basil leaves with the tomatoes, and arrange them on a platter or individual plates, layering them with the tomato-soaked croutons and dollops of the ricotta. Finish with a drizzle of the remaining tomato juice and serve.

SUGGESTIONS FOR TOMATOES:

Spicy Bloody Mary
Place 1 pound coarsely chopped tomatoes, ½ chile pepper, 1 celery stalk, a coarsely chopped small onion, and a dash of Worcestershire sauce in a blender and puree until smooth. Pass through a sieve and serve over iced vodka. Garnish with celery hearts.

Quick and Easy Pasta Sauce
Blanch 6 large tomatoes in boiling water for 30 seconds. Cool under cold running water and peel. Coarsely chop the tomatoes and mix with 1 minced garlic clove, a small handful of pitted black olives, a small handful of coarsely torn fresh basil, and a teaspoon of capers. Place in a saucepan and warm through. Add freshly cooked hot pasta, such as spaghetti or penne. Serve with grated Parmesan cheese.

Salsa
Blanch 4 tomatoes in boiling water for 30 seconds. Cool under cold running water. Then peel, quarter, and seed the tomatoes, and place in a bowl. Add ¼ teaspoon chopped hot chile, ½ teaspoon minced garlic, half a small red onion, finely diced, a small handful of coarsely chopped fresh cilantro, a generous squeeze of lime juice, and a slug of olive oil. Season with sea salt to taste. Toss well and serve over grilled fish, chicken, or steak.

Gazpacho
Blanch 1 pound ripe tomatoes in boiling water for 30 seconds. Cool under cold running water. Then peel and chop the tomatoes. In a bowl, combine the tomatoes with 6 ounces stale bread crumbs. Add 1 chopped, seeded, peeled cucumber, 2 chopped garlic cloves, 1 red and 1 yellow chopped, seeded bell pepper, 3 to 4 tablespoons red wine vinegar, 4 tablespoons olive oil, and sea salt and pepper to taste. Stir well, then puree, in batches, in a blender with approximately 2 cups ice water. Chill and serve with a garnish of chopped scallions, cucumber, red bell peppers, and croutons.

MARINATED SALMON AND FENNEL SALAD
WITH MUSTARD-DILL DRESSING

This is an elegant appetizer that is easy to put together at the last minute because the salmon is prepared 3 to 5 days ahead. Curing the salmon draws the fluids out of the fish, intensifying the flavor and adding a subtle sweetness and saltiness.

I am a huge fan of fennel because of its strong anise flavor. It goes particularly well with the cured salmon, but try it also with other fish and meat, especially pork and veal. If you are not keen on the flavor, serve the salmon with a potato salad: Boil new potatoes in salted water until al dente and then marinate in olive oil, lemon zest and juice, and chopped fresh mint. Add some sliced raw sugar snap peas for crunchy texture and sweetness. SERVES 10 AS AN APPETIZER

SALMON

2 tablespoons fennel seeds

2 tablespoons coarse sea salt

2 tablespoons sugar

1 teaspoon black peppercorns, crushed

1 teaspoon grated orange zest

2 tablespoons coarsely chopped fennel fronds

2 tablespoons coarsely chopped fresh mint leaves

2 pounds salmon fillet, skin on, cut from the middle part of the fillet

1 tablespoon Pernod, optional

FENNEL SALAD

1 to 2 bulbs fennel, tough outer layer removed

1 teaspoon chopped fennel fronds

1 tablespoon extra virgin olive oil

Sea salt and freshly ground pepper

1 tablespoon small capers

¼ cup fresh flat-leaf parsley leaves

½ red onion, thinly sliced

1 bunch salad greens (watercress, upland cress, or pea shoots)

1 recipe Mustard-Dill Dressing (page 93)

Whole-grain bread, thinly sliced and toasted

Prepare the salmon: Mix the fennel seeds, sea salt, sugar, peppercorns, orange zest, fennel fronds, and mint in a small bowl. Rub this mixture over the salmon flesh. If you are using the Pernod, sprinkle it over the salmon. Wrap the salmon in plastic wrap and place it on a baking sheet. Place a second baking sheet on the fish, then top with heavy objects, such as bottles or cans, to weight it down. Refrigerate for at least 3 days and up to 5.

When you are ready to serve the salad, unwrap the salmon and gently scrape off the excess marinade. Place the salmon on a clean cutting board and cut it into paper-thin slices.

Slice the fennel as thin as possible, using a mandoline if you have one, and place it in a bowl. Add the fennel fronds, olive oil, and a pinch of sea salt and pepper. Toss together, coating the fennel evenly.

Combine the capers, parsley, and red onions in another bowl, and season with a pinch of sea salt and pepper.

Arrange the salad greens on individual plates and drape the sliced salmon loosely over the top. Place the fennel to one side on the plate and scatter the onion-caper mixture over the salmon. Drizzle with the Mustard-Dill Dressing and serve with the whole-grain toast.

MUSTARD-DILL DRESSING   MAKES 2 CUPS

3 teaspoons fennel seeds, toasted

½ cup Dijon mustard

1 teaspoon dry mustard

4 tablespoons super-fine sugar

½ cup white wine vinegar

1 cup extra virgin olive oil

4 teaspoons coarsely chopped fresh dill

Grind the fennel seeds in a mortar and pestle and then combine them in a bowl with the mustards, sugar, and vinegar. Slowly add the olive oil, beating well until the dressing has emulsified to a thick and creamy consistency. Stir in the chopped dill.

SHRIMP AND CUCUMBER SALAD
WITH DILL CRÈME FRAÎCHE

Most shrimp available in the supermarket have been frozen. This doesn't necessarily suggest they are not good quality. Shrimp are often frozen on the fishing vessel immediately after being caught, thus retaining their freshness and firm texture. The supermarkets then defrost the shrimp and advertise them as fresh.

The best way to buy shrimp is to purchase them alive. I am fortunate to live close to New York's Chinatown, where shrimp are sold live from a tank. Carrying live shrimp home is an experience, but well worth the strange looks from passers by as your shopping bag jumps and bites!

Once you are home, put the live shrimp in the freezer for about 10 minutes to anesthetize them. Then plunge them into boiling water for a couple of minutes, or until their shells turn a reddish color. Drain and cool before peeling. (Cooking them in their shells helps retain their sweet juices.) When they are as fresh as this, you can serve them simply with aioli, sea salt, and lemon.

The shrimp and dressing can be made 4 hours ahead of time, making this an easy salad to put together.   SERVES 4 AS AN APPETIZER

8 cups water

Sea salt

1 pound large shrimp, unpeeled

Freshly ground black pepper

Grated zest of 1 lemon

1 teaspoon coarsely chopped fresh dill

1 teaspoon coarsely chopped fresh chervil

1 tablespoon extra virgin olive oil

Place the water in a large, heavy saucepan, add a generous pinch of sea salt, and bring to a boil. Add the shrimp, give them a stir, and boil until just cooked through, 2 to 3 minutes. (Most varieties of shrimp will turn orange or reddish when cooked.) Drain, spread the shrimp out on a plate, and allow to cool.

When they are cool enough to handle, remove the shrimp heads and shells. (You may want to save these for fish stock.) Devein the shrimp by slitting the length of the top of the shrimp and removing the black vein. Place the shrimp in a bowl, season with sea salt and pepper to taste, and add the lemon zest, dill, chervil, and olive oil. Toss well to coat the shrimp evenly. If you are not serving them right away, cover and refrigerate until ready to use.

DRESSING

½ English (hothouse) cucumber,
   peeled

¼ cup crème fraîche

2 tablespoons yogurt

2 teaspoons lemon juice

Pinch cayenne pepper, plus extra for
   garnish

¼ teaspoon minced garlic

3 scallions (white parts only), thinly
   sliced on the diagonal

1 teaspoon coarsely chopped
   fresh dill

Sea salt

4 handfuls salad greens, such as pea
   shoots, watercress, or romaine
   lettuce

Prepare the dressing: Cut the cucumber in half lengthwise and, using a teaspoon, scrape out any seeds. Cut the cucumber halves into diagonal half-moon slices.

Place the crème fraîche, yogurt, lemon juice, cayenne, garlic, scallions, dill, and sea salt to taste in a bowl and mix well. Fold in the sliced cucumber. Taste and adjust the seasoning if necessary. The dressing should be a stiff pouring consistency. Add a little more lemon juice or a splash of water if it is too thick.

When ready to serve, divide the salad greens among four plates and arrange the shrimp on top. Spoon the dressing attractively around the shrimp and finish with a sprinkle of cayenne pepper.

ROASTED PEPPER, EGGPLANT, CIPOLLINE, AND MOZZARELLA SALAD

This dish consists of a selection of tastes and textures that complement each other. It makes for an ideal introduction to a dinner party, as it awakens the palate with its bold and pungent flavors. The peppers and onions exude sweetness, while the olives and eggplant offer saltiness and spice. Creamy smooth mozzarella lends itself well to all of these flavors. Turn this into a main course by adding sliced prosciutto, ham, and salami. Each of the components of this dish can be prepared ahead and refrigerated. SERVES 4

PEPPERS

2 red bell peppers

1 yellow bell pepper

2 tablespoons extra virgin olive oil

¼ teaspoon minced garlic

Sea salt and freshly ground black
    pepper

EGGPLANT

2 large eggplants (about 1½ pounds
    total)

½ cup thick yogurt, such as Greek
    yogurt (see Note)

½ small clove garlic, minced

¼ teaspoon finely chopped hot chile
    pepper, such as Thai

1 tablespoon lemon juice

Small bunch cilantro, coarsely
    chopped, including stems

Sea salt

ONIONS

2 tablespoons olive oil

1 clove garlic

1 pound cipolline onions, spring onion
    bulbs, scallions, or shallots

2 sprigs thyme

Sea salt

PREPARE THE PEPPERS:

Preheat the oven to 375°F.

Place the peppers in an ovenproof dish and smear them with 1 tablespoon of the olive oil. Roast until the pepper skins begin to darken, approximately 20 minutes. Remove from the oven and set aside to cool.

When they are cool enough to handle, peel off the skins. Carefully open the peppers with your hands and remove the seeds. Then tear them into bite-size pieces. Place the peppers in a bowl, add the remaining 1 tablespoon olive oil, the garlic, and sea salt and pepper to taste, and toss to mix.

PREPARE THE EGGPLANT:

Preheat the oven to 375°F.

Place the eggplants on a baking sheet, and using a fork, prick the skin half a dozen times (this prevents the eggplant from exploding while baking). Bake the eggplant in the oven until the flesh is soft, approximately 40 minutes. (To test, carefully squeeze the eggplant; there should be no resistance.) Remove the eggplants from the oven and set them aside to cool.

When they are cool enough to handle, cut the eggplants in half and scrape out the flesh, discarding the skins. Put the flesh into a mixing bowl and add the yogurt, garlic, chile, lemon juice, cilantro, and a pinch of sea salt. Stir well, taste, and adjust the seasoning as needed. Add extra chile pepper or garlic if you like it really pungent.

PREPARE THE ONIONS:

Preheat the oven to 350°F.

Heat the olive oil in an ovenproof sauté pan over medium heat. Add the garlic and sauté, while gently shaking the pan, until it begins to turn golden brown, about 5 minutes. Then remove it with a slotted spoon and discard it. Add the onions and the thyme

MOZZARELLA

8 ounces imported Italian buffalo
mozzarella, cut into 8 wedges

Splash of extra virgin olive oil

Sea salt and freshly ground black
pepper

BLACK OLIVE AND PARSLEY RELISH

1 cup black olives, such as Niçoise or
Gaeta, pitted

½ cup fresh flat-leaf parsley leaves

1 teaspoon small capers

Grated zest of 1 lemon

Smidgeon minced garlic

1 tablespoon extra virgin olive oil

Arugula leaves, for garnish

Bread sticks

to the pan and sauté, gently shaking the pan, until the onions are golden brown, 5 minutes. Transfer the sauté pan to the oven and roast the onions until they are tender, 15 to 20 minutes. Remove from the oven and set aside to cool.

PREPARE THE MOZZARELLA:

Place the cheese in a bowl and drizzle with the olive oil. Season with sea salt and pepper to taste, and set aside.

PREPARE THE RELISH:

Place the olives, parsley, capers, lemon zest, garlic, and olive oil in a bowl, and stir to mix well.

ASSEMBLE THE DISH:

Allow all the components to come to room temperature. Arrange the roasted peppers, eggplant mixture, roasted onions, marinated mozzarella, and olive-parsley relish on a large platter or on individual plates. Garnish with arugula leaves and serve with bread sticks.

NOTE:

To thicken yogurt, fit a coffee filter or a piece of muslin inside a strainer and set it over a bowl. Place the yogurt in the filter and set the bowl in the refrigerator for as little as 30 minutes or as long as overnight. The longer you strain it, the thicker the yogurt will be.

B.L.T.

Sandwich naturally cured bacon with summer-ripe heirloom tomatoes and a crisp lettuce leaf between slices of hearty country bread, and you've reached a state of euphoria in the sandwich world!   MAKES 1 SANDWICH

4 slices naturally cured bacon, rind removed

1 large heirloom tomato, cored and sliced

1 teaspoon extra virgin olive oil

Smidgeon minced garlic

Sea salt and freshly ground black pepper

2 slices country-style bread

Prepared English mustard, optional

2 crisp romaine or Bibb lettuce leaves

Preheat the oven to 370°F.

Place the bacon on a baking sheet and bake until crisp, about 10 minutes. Set the bacon aside.

Place the tomato slices in a mixing bowl and toss gently with the olive oil, garlic, and sea salt and pepper to taste. Let this sit for 10 to 15 minutes to encourage the tomatoes to release their delicious natural juices. Stir every so often, basting the tomatoes in their juice.

Toast the bread. If you are using mustard, spread it over one side of a piece of toast. Arrange the lettuce on top, followed by the bacon and tomatoes. Spoon the tomato juices over the top. Put the second slice of bread on top, cut in half, and eat!

MOROCCAN CHICKEN ON CORIANDER FLAT BREAD WITH CARROT AND ALMOND SALAD

This recipe makes more than enough of the warm Moroccan-style spice blend that flavors the chicken. The extra will keep well in a sealed container in the refrigerator for up to 5 days. Use it to marinate meat or fish—it is especially good rubbed over a leg of lamb before slow roasting, or over a whole fish such as dorade or snapper. Don't be overly concerned with following the exact quantities of ingredients when preparing the spice mixture; add as much or as little of the various spices as you prefer. Taste the mix before you rub it into the chicken; it should be pungent, spicy, and fresh-tasting.

I like flat bread for this sandwich because its texture lends itself well to the spice paste, soaking up the juices from the chicken. You could also use store-bought pita bread or tortillas. MAKES 2 SANDWICHES

MOROCCAN SPICE MIX

1 tablespoon cumin seeds, ground

1 teaspoon saffron threads

1 teaspoon paprika

1 bunch cilantro

3 cloves garlic

1/2 teaspoon chopped hot chile pepper, such as Thai

1 tablespoon ground ginger

Grated zest of 1 lemon

5 tablespoons lemon juice

6 tablespoons extra virgin olive oil

1/4 teaspoon sea salt

2 whole boneless chicken breasts, skin on

1 tablespoon extra virgin olive oil

2 large carrots, coarsely grated

1 tablespoon slivered almonds, toasted

1 tablespoon golden raisins

2 tablespoons orange juice

1 tablespoon lemon juice

1/4 teaspoon ground cinnamon

1/3 cup fresh cilantro leaves

1/3 cup fresh mint leaves

(continued)

Prepare the spice mix: Place the cumin, saffron, and paprika in a sauté pan and toast over low heat until fragrant, 2 to 3 minutes. Transfer the mixture to a food processor and add the cilantro, garlic, chile, ginger, lemon zest, lemon juice, olive oil, and salt. Puree to a smooth paste.

Spread 2 tablespoons of the spice mix over the chicken breasts and place in a baking dish. Cover and refrigerate for at least 2 hours and up to 24 hours. (Reserve the remaining spice mix for another use.)

Heat the olive oil in a sauté pan over medium heat. Add the chicken breasts, skin side down, and cook until the skin is crisp and golden brown, 5 to 6 minutes. Do not raise the heat, as it will burn the spice mix. Turn the chicken over and cook the other side for approximately 5 minutes. (To test if the chicken is cooked, press the thickest part of the flesh with your fingers. The flesh should be fairly firm, showing slight resistance to the touch. If it is soft, the chicken is undercooked.) Alternatively, you could cook the chicken on a preheated grill, omitting the olive oil.

Remove the chicken from the pan and allow it to cool slightly.

Meanwhile, prepare the salad by placing the carrots in a bowl and adding the almonds, raisins, orange and lemon juices, cinnamon, cilantro, and mint. Season with a pinch of sea salt and black pepper to taste.

Preheat the oven to 425°F or prepare a hot grill.

Place the flat bread dough on a lightly floured surface. Sprinkle the dough with the coriander seeds and knead it for 1 to 2 minutes, until the seeds are distributed evenly and the dough is smooth. Cut two 3-ounce pieces from the dough and roll them into 8-inch rounds.

Place the rounds on the highest rack in the oven or directly onto the grill. Bake until the bread starts to bubble, rise, and turn golden brown, 1 to 2 minutes. Then carefully, using

Sea salt and freshly ground black pepper

6 ounces risen flat bread dough (page 221), or 2 store-bought pita breads

1 teaspoon coriander seeds, toasted and coarsely crushed

Small handful arugula leaves, trimmed

a pair of tongs, flip the bread over and cook the other side for 1 to 2 minutes. Be careful not to overcook the bread, or it will become too brittle to fold.

The remaining dough can be covered and stored in the refrigerator for 24 hours, or divided into 6 additional pieces, rolled out, baked, and stored in an airtight container. (If using store-bought bread, simply place it in the oven or on the grill to heat through.)

Slice the chicken. Place some arugula on one half of each bread and layer the chicken over the arugula. Arrange the carrot and almond salad across the top. Fold the other half of the bread over to form a sandwich.

TUNA CIABATTA WITH ONION–PINE NUT RELISH

The combination of grilled onions marinated with raisins, orange juice, and olive oil is a wonderful blend of sweet and savory essences that pairs beautifully with tuna. This is a superb sandwich to serve in the summer—it's healthy, light, fruity, and easy to cook on the grill. MAKES 4 SANDWICHES

RELISH

Small handful golden raisins

Grated zest of 1 orange

1 cup fresh orange juice

1 hot chile pepper, such as jalapeño or Thai, finely chopped

2 tablespoons balsamic vinegar

2 white onions, sliced into generous ¼-inch-thick rings (try to keep the rings intact for easier grilling)

2 tablespoons extra virgin olive oil

Sea salt and freshly ground black pepper

3 tablespoons pine nuts, toasted

2 tablespoons fresh flat-leaf parsley leaves

1 tablespoon extra virgin olive oil

Four 4-ounce tuna steaks, skin removed

4 ciabatta rolls, or other similar rolls

4 tablespoons aioli (page 24)

1 bunch watercress, trimmed

PREPARE THE RELISH:

Place the raisins in a bowl and add the orange zest and juice, chile, and balsamic vinegar; stir well. Leave the raisins to soak in this marinade for at least 30 minutes.

Prepare a hot grill.

Place the onion rings on the grill rack and grill for approximately 4 minutes (depending on the ferocity of the heat); then turn the rings over and grill on the other side until the onions are charred and are beginning to soften. Transfer the onions to the bowl containing the raisins, stir in the olive oil and season with sea salt and pepper to taste. Stir well and cover the bowl to steam the onions for 20 minutes (to ensure they are tender).

Just before you put the tuna on the grill, stir the pine nuts and parsley leaves into the onion mixture.

GRILL THE TUNA:

Smear the olive oil over the tuna steaks and season them with sea salt and pepper.

Place the tuna over the hottest part of the grill and cook to your taste. The cooking time will vary according to the thickness of the tuna: approximately 30 seconds on each side for rare, 1 to 2 minutes on each side for medium-rare, 2 to 3 minutes on each side for medium, and 5 minutes on each side for well-done.

ASSEMBLE THE SANDWICH:

Cut the ciabatta rolls in half and warm them on the grill. Spread the aioli on the inside of the warmed rolls. Divide the watercress among the bottom halves and place the cooked tuna on top. Finish with a generous spoonful of onion–pine nut relish, allowing the orange-flavored juices to soak into the bread. Set the top halves in place and serve.

TUNA BURGERS WITH AVOCADO RELISH

I like to cook my tuna burgers rare; this helps retain the juice and accentuates the seasonings—lots of chile, garlic, onion, and lime. (Note that you can prepare the burgers 8 to 12 hours in advance.)

Try serving the burgers with fried plantain chips: Peel a plantain, cut it into thin lengthwise slices on a mandoline, then deep-fry in vegetable oil until crisp and golden brown. Season with sea salt and freshly ground black pepper. These can be made up to 48 hours in advance if stored in an airtight container. SERVES 4

1½ pounds tuna loin, skinless

4 scallions (white part only), finely sliced

½ cup finely diced red onion

¼ teaspoon chopped hot chile pepper, such as jalapeño or Thai

1 teaspoon minced garlic

1 cup chopped fresh cilantro

1 teaspoon grated lemon zest

1 teaspoon grated lime zest

2 tablespoons lime juice

Sea salt and freshly ground black pepper

1 tablespoon extra virgin olive oil

4 hamburger buns, brioche buns, or English muffins

4 small handfuls arugula leaves

1 recipe Avocado Relish (page 107)

Fill a large metal bowl halfway with ice cubes. Set a medium-size metal bowl on top of the ice.

Cut the tuna into ¼-inch dice and place it in the medium-size bowl. (This will help maintain the temperature of the fish while you season it.) Add the scallions, red onions, chile, garlic, cilantro, lemon and lime zests, and lime juice. Add a generous pinch of sea salt and pepper, and stir well to incorporate all the ingredients.

Line four 1-inch-deep, 3½-inch-diameter ring molds or cookie cutters with plastic wrap, overlapping the edges. Using a dessert spoon, pack the tuna mixture into the molds, compressing it firmly with the back of the spoon. Fold the overlapping edges of plastic wrap over the tuna, covering it completely, and then carefully remove the ring mold. Place the burgers in the refrigerator for up to 12 hours.

Heat the olive oil in a sauté pan over medium heat. Remove the plastic wrap from the burgers, place them in the pan, and cook for approximately 2 minutes. Then turn them over and cook for 2 minutes for medium-rare (this will depend upon the thickness of the burgers). If you prefer them cooked a little more, continue to sauté them for another minute on each side.

While the burgers are cooking, preheat the broiler.

Cut the buns in half and toast them on both sides under the broiler.

Arrange the arugula leaves over the bottom half of each bun. Place the tuna burgers on top and finish with a generous spoonful of the Avocado Relish. Set the top halves in place and serve immediately.

AVOCADO RELISH   MAKES 1½ CUPS

2 ripe avocados

2 tablespoons lime juice

1 teaspoon grated lime zest

¼ teaspoon chopped hot chile

½ teaspoon minced garlic

⅓ cup finely diced red onion

1 tablespoon coarsely chopped fresh cilantro

1 tablespoon extra virgin olive oil

¼ teaspoon sea salt

Slice the avocados into strips or cubes and place them in a medium-size mixing bowl. Add the lime juice, lime zest, chile, garlic, red onions, cilantro, and olive oil. Season with sea salt to taste.

ZEST

When zesting citrus fruit, do not press the fruit too hard against the zester or grater, or it will cut into the bitter white pith beneath the zest. You want just the colored outside layer of the peel.

WARM EGGPLANT, MOZZARELLA, AND PESTO SANDWICH

Pesto, a rich and fragrant sauce that originated in Genoa, Italy, is made with basil, garlic, toasted pine nuts, Parmesan or pecorino cheese, and olive oil. Today pesto has a cult following, with many versions ranging from feta and almond pesto to sundried tomato and walnut pesto. The recipe here is the traditional one, but by all means experiment and devise your own style of pesto.

Use ciabatta or focaccia for this sandwich, as its irregular texture is great for soaking up the olive oil and juices from the eggplant and pesto. MAKES 2 SANDWICHES

½ cup extra virgin olive oil, plus more for grilling

1 teaspoon chopped fresh rosemary

½ teaspoon minced garlic

Sea salt and freshly ground black pepper

Six ¼-inch-thick slices eggplant

2 pieces focaccia or ciabatta

4 slices buffalo mozzarella

1 recipe Pesto (page 109)

Prepare a hot grill. Mix the olive oil, rosemary, garlic, and a pinch of sea salt and pepper in a bowl. Using your hands or a pastry brush, coat the sliced eggplant with this marinade. Be careful not to end up with excess oil on the eggplant, as it will burn over the flames. Keep any leftover oil for smearing on the bread.

Grill the eggplant for 3 to 4 minutes on each side.

Alternatively you can sauté the eggplant by heating a tablespoon of olive oil (you may need more, as the eggplant acts as a sponge, soaking up the oil) in a sauté pan over medium heat. Add the eggplant slices in a single layer, and cook until golden brown and tender, 3 to 4 minutes on each side.

Remove the eggplant from the heat and set it aside.

To assemble the sandwiches, cut the focaccia or ciabatta in half horizontally, and layer in the eggplant and sliced mozzarella on one half. Finish with a generous spoonful of pesto and place the other half of the bread on top. Smear the outside of the bread with any remaining olive oil, and place the sandwiches on the grill or in a sauté pan. (You may need to add a touch of olive oil to the sauté pan.) Press the sandwiches with a spatula, and cook until they are golden brown on both sides and the mozzarella has started to soften and melt, about 4 minutes. Remove the sandwiches from the heat, cut them in half, and serve.

PESTO MAKES 1/4 CUP

2 tablespoons extra virgin olive oil

1 tablespoon pine nuts

Few slivers garlic

Sea salt and freshly ground black pepper

Generous handful fresh basil leaves

1 tablespoon freshly grated Parmesan cheese

Heat 1 tablespoon of the olive oil in a sauté pan with the pine nuts over medium heat. Cook until they turn golden brown, about 2 minutes. Remove from the heat and allow to cool.

Mash the garlic in a mortar and pestle with a good pinch of sea salt and pepper. Add the basil and continue to pound until evenly crushed. Then add the toasted pine nuts and continue to bash until you have a fairly smooth mixture. Slowly add the remaining 1 tablespoon olive oil, stirring constantly, and then stir in the cheese. Taste and adjust the seasoning if necessary. (You can also make this in a food processor by combining all the ingredients and pureeing until smooth.) The pesto will keep for 2 to 3 days in an airtight jar in the refrigerator.

LEMON ICE CREAM SANDWICH
WITH BLUEBERRY COMPOTE

Of course you can buy your favorite brand of ice cream for this dessert, but where's the fun in that? Make this homemade ice cream at least a day in advance to ensure that it will be firm enough to cut into rounds.

I have paired the lemon ice cream with a lavender shortbread. This super-fragrant flower adds an unusual perfumed flavor to the rich shortbread. During the summer months you will find lavender at farmers' markets. If you are not able to find it fresh, you can find it dried at specialty food stores.

The ice cream, shortbread, and blueberry compote can all be prepared in advance, but don't assemble the sandwiches until you are ready to serve them. MAKES ABOUT 10 SANDWICHES

ICE CREAM

1 cup lemon juice (about 8 lemons)

1 cup superfine sugar

2 cups light cream

1 vanilla bean

10 large egg yolks

Grated zest of 3 lemons

2½ cups heavy cream

SHORTBREAD

1 tablespoon fresh or dried lavender
  flowers

⅓ cup light brown sugar

8 tablespoons (1 stick) unsalted butter

1 large egg, beaten (3 tablespoons)

½ teaspoon vanilla extract

1¼ cups all-purpose flour

½ teaspoon salt

Grated zest of 1 lemon

Confectioners' sugar, for dusting

1 recipe Blueberry Compote
  (page 114)

PREPARE THE ICE CREAM:

Combine the lemon juice and ½ cup of the superfine sugar in a saucepan and simmer over medium heat until the mixture has reduced by half and has the consistency of syrup. Remove from the heat and set aside.

Place the light cream in a heavy-bottomed saucepan. Split the vanilla bean in half lengthwise and scrape out the seeds with a small knife. Add the pod and seeds to the cream and cook over moderate heat until just below the boiling point. Remove the pan from the heat and set it aside to allow the vanilla to infuse the cream.

Mix the egg yolks, remaining ½ cup sugar, and the lemon zest in a large bowl until pale and thick. Remove the vanilla pods and slowly pour the warm cream into the egg mixture, stirring continually to prevent the eggs from curdling. Return this mixture to the pan, and stirring slowly and constantly, heat it until it starts to thicken and form a custard that will coat the back of the spoon, 6 to 8 minutes. Then stir in the lemon syrup and remove the pan from the heat. Pass the mixture through a fine-mesh sieve into a bowl, stir in the heavy cream, and allow to cool completely.

Churn the ice cream in an ice cream maker, following the manufacturer's instructions. Then transfer it to a 1-inch-deep pan that is approximately 12 by 9 inches, cover it, and place it in the freezer to set overnight.

Once the ice cream is firm, use a 1-inch-deep, 2½-inch-diameter cookie cutter to cut out rounds of ice cream. Return the rounds to the freezer until ready to use.

PREPARE THE SHORTBREAD:

Place the lavender and the brown sugar in a food processor and pulse to incorporate. Add the butter and process until light and creamy. Add the egg and vanilla extract, and process until blended. Then add the flour, salt, and lemon zest, and process until it forms a dough. Remove the dough from the processor onto a lightly floured surface, and using your hands, form two logs approximately 1½ inches in diameter. Let the dough logs rest for at least 30 minutes in the refrigerator. The logs will keep for up to 1 week wrapped in plastic.

Preheat the oven to 350°F. Line two baking sheets with parchment paper.

Cut the dough logs into ¼-inch-thick rounds and place them on the prepared baking sheets. Bake until golden and firm, approximately 12 minutes. Remove the cookies to a wire rack to cool. Store them in an airtight container for up to 2 days.

TO ASSEMBLE AND SERVE THE SANDWICHES:

Use a spatula to transfer each ice cream round onto a cookie and sandwich with another cookie. Dust with confectioners' sugar and serve immediately with the Blueberry Compote on the side.

BLUEBERRY COMPOTE   MAKES 1½ CUPS

¾ pound blueberries
Grated zest of 1 orange
Juice of 2 oranges
3 tablespoons superfine sugar
5 tablespoons water
Splash Grand Marnier, optional

Combine all the ingredients in a saucepan and bring to a simmer over medium heat. Cover the pan, lower the heat, and simmer until the blueberries start to collapse and the released juices have thickened, approximately 10 minutes. Remove from the pan and allow to cool. The compote can be prepared up to 2 days ahead, covered and refrigerated. Warm it before serving.

AUTUMN

SOUPS

Mushroom and Tarragon Soup

Squash Soup with Roasted Chestnuts and Pancetta

Celeriac, Apple, and Stilton Soup with
Apple-Sage Muffins

Cannellini Bean, Prosciutto, and Mustard Greens Soup

Spiced Parsnip Soup with Crunchy Parsnip Chips

Spicy Mussel and Tomato Soup

SALADS

Prosciutto, Walnut, and Goat Cheese Salad

Roasted Duck Breast with Red Mustard Leaf and Fig Salad

Mushroom and Parmesan Salad with
Lemon-Chive Dressing

Roasted Autumn Vegetable Salad with
Maple-Cider Dressing

Crab Salad with Pickled Eggplant,
Shaved Fennel, and Radish

Pomegranate-Glazed Quail with
Cinnamon-Raisin Tabbouleh

SANDWICHES

Warm Prosciutto, Mushroom, Taleggio, and Spinach Sandwich

Lancashire Cheese Sandwich
with Fig Chutney

Gorgonzola, Pear, and Honey Open-Faced Sandwich

Ricotta, Fig, and Pistachio Panettone

Sausage, Mushroom, and Melted Cheese Sandwiches

Smoked Salmon and Scrambled Egg Bagel

The autumn season is gently broken in with a flourish of late-summer tomatoes, egg-plants, corn, shallots, flowering herbs, and plums. If you are lucky, a second growing of raspberries and strawberries may appear. As we approach October, winter squash and pumpkins, new varieties of mushrooms, celery root, parsnips, and shellfish are in full swing. There is also an abundance of wonderful fruits—blackberries, figs, and numerous varieties of grapes, apples, and pears, not to mention the jewel-like seeds of the pome-granate. It's also time for nut cracking; look for fresh chestnuts, walnuts, hazelnuts, and pecans.

The recipes in this chapter represent the lingering crossover of summer into autumn, encompassing warm, earthy flavors. As autumn progresses, it supports richer foods. The body is ready for heartier dishes, such as squash soup with chestnuts and pancetta. The sandwiches focus on cheese, celebrating its rich and unctuous melting qualities—and in some cases, its rather strong smelling qualities! You will meet a cheesemaker from Lan-cashire, England, whose passion and dedication are something to be admired.

ITEMS FOUND IN ABUNDANCE IN AUTUMN:

Apples
Broccoli
Carrots
Celery
Celery root
Chestnuts
Grapes
Greens
Mushrooms
Nuts
Onions
Parsnips
Pears
Pecans
Pomegranates
Quince
Radishes
Rutabagas
Shellfish
Turnips

MUSHROOM AND TARRAGON SOUP

This soup can be made with a variety of mushrooms. Try the buttery and sweet-tasting chestnut mushroom, also known as cremini. It is similar to the white button mushroom but with a deeper, earthier flavor. Or try the more delicate oyster mushroom. Puffball mushrooms, gathered at the end of the summer and beginning of autumn, have an ideal texture for this recipe. The common portobello and the wild field mushroom both have a deep meatiness and, once pureed, add a velvety texture.

SERVES 4 TO 6

1 bunch tarragon

5 tablespoons unsalted butter

1 tablespoon extra virgin olive oil

2 cloves garlic, green shoot removed, minced

1 large onion, coarsely chopped

1 stalk celery, coarsely chopped

2 pounds mushrooms, trimmed (trimmings reserved) and quartered, plus 6 whole mushrooms

Sea salt and freshly ground black pepper

1 recipe Mushroom Stock (page 122)

1 cup heavy cream

8 tablespoons freshly grated Parmesan cheese, optional

Remove the tarragon leaves from their stems, reserving both separately. Melt 4 tablespoons of the butter with the olive oil in a large saucepan over medium heat. When it starts to sizzle, add the tarragon stems, garlic, onions, and celery. Stir to coat in the butter, and sauté for about 5 minutes. Then add the mushrooms, season generously with sea salt and pepper, and continue to sauté until the mushrooms start to brown, 5 to 10 minutes. Add the mushroom stock and bring to a boil. Lower the heat and simmer gently until the vegetables are tender, approximately 35 minutes.

Remove the pan from the heat. Ladle the soup, in batches, into a blender and puree until smooth. Push the puree through a sieve into a clean saucepan and discard the solids. (At this point if you are not serving the soup immediately, you can transfer it to a container and store it in the refrigerator 3 to 4 days.)

Coarsely chop two thirds of the tarragon leaves and add them, along with the heavy cream, to the soup. Warm it over low heat, stirring constantly for 5 to 10 minutes. If the soup seems too thick, add more stock or water.

Keep the pot on the stove but turn the heat off. Add the Parmesan cheese, if desired, stirring until it has melted.

Prepare the garnish: Slice the reserved whole mushrooms and sauté them in the remaining tablespoon of butter until golden brown, 5 minutes. Season to taste with sea salt and pepper.

Spoon the hot soup into warmed bowls and arrange the sautéed mushrooms on top. Garnish with the remaining tarragon leaves.

MUSHROOM STOCK   MAKES 6 CUPS

1 tablespoon olive oil

2 handfuls trimmings from mushrooms used for soup

3 cloves garlic, minced

2 sprigs thyme, sage, or rosemary

Generous pinch sea salt

8 cups water

Heat the olive oil in a saucepan over medium heat. Add the mushroom trimmings and sauté until golden brown, 5 minutes. Add the garlic, thyme sprigs, and sea salt. Then add the water and bring to a boil. Lower the heat and simmer until the mushrooms have released their flavor and the liquid has reduced to approximately 6 cups, 15 to 20 minutes.

Pass the the contents through a sieve into a bowl, pushing on them with a spoon to extract as much flavor as possible. Discard the solids and set the stock aside to cool. The stock can be stored in the refrigerator for 3 to 4 days or frozen for later use.

TARRAGON

This strongly flavored herb awakens the palate. Here are some ideas:

- *Boil or steam new potatoes until tender. Drain, then toss in a mixture of crème fraîche, coarsely chopped fresh tarragon, sea salt, and pepper.*

- *Blanch a variety of young vegetables, such as carrots, green and yellow beans, zucchini, and fennel; drain and let them cool. Then marinate in a mixture of olive oil, minced garlic, grated lemon zest, and fresh tarragon. Serve as a salad to accompany poached salmon.*

- *Add tarragon stems to a saucepan of chicken stock and simmer until reduced. Pass through a fine-mesh sieve and return to a clean saucepan. Add a splash of heavy cream and reduce until a sauce consistency is achieved. Stir in coarsely chopped tarragon and spoon over grilled or poached chicken breasts.*

- *Make a flavored butter to serve on grilled meat or fish: Place softened butter in a bowl and add finely diced shallots, coarsely chopped tarragon, minced garlic, a pinch of cayenne, coarsely chopped capers, minced anchovy fillet, and prepared mustard. Stir until well blended. Place a teaspoonful over each portion of meat or fish, allowing it to melt before serving.*

MUSHROOMS

- Purchase mushrooms that are firm and dry. Make sure the gills are unbroken and the flesh is not scratched or damaged.

- If the mushrooms are very soiled, use a paring knife or a small brush to scrape off the excess dirt, or wipe the mushrooms with a dry cloth. If this doesn't do the trick, quickly toss the mushrooms in a bowl of cold water and then dry them in a salad spinner or spread them out on a clean cloth near a cool draft to dry.

- Store mushrooms in a perforated paper bag or wrap them in newspaper, and place them in the refrigerator. They should keep for 4 to 5 days.

SQUASH SOUP WITH ROASTED CHESTNUTS AND PANCETTA

This warming autumnal soup, with its chunky texture and savory flavor, is quick and easy, making it an ideal meal when you are strapped for time. SERVES 6

4 tablespoons (½ stick) butter

1 tablespoon extra virgin olive oil, plus extra for drizzling

One ¼-inch-thick slice pancetta, cut into strips

1 stalk celery, halved lengthwise and diced

2 pounds butternut squash, peeled, seeded, and cut into ½-inch cubes

1 onion, finely diced

2 cloves garlic, minced

12 fresh sage leaves, coarsely chopped

10 bottled roasted chestnuts, coarsely chopped

2½ cups Vegetable Stock (page 225), chicken stock, or water

Sea salt and freshly ground black pepper

12 shavings Parmesan cheese (shaved with a vegetable peeler)

Handful croutons (see page 191)

Melt the butter with the olive oil in a large saucepan over medium heat. Add the pancetta and celery and sauté for 10 minutes, stirring every so often. Add the squash, onions, and garlic, and continue to sauté for another 5 minutes. Stir in the sage and chestnuts, add the stock, season with sea salt and pepper to taste, and bring to a boil. Lower the heat and simmer until the vegetables are tender and the squash has started to collapse, about 15 minutes.

Divide the soup among six individual warmed bowls. Drizzle a little olive oil over the top of each portion and garnish with the shaved Parmesan. Offer the croutons on the side. Serve immediately.

NOTE:

If you are not serving the soup straightaway, you may need to add more water or stock when you reheat it, as the squash has a tendency to soak up the liquid, making it very thick.

CELERIAC, APPLE, AND STILTON SOUP
WITH APPLE-SAGE MUFFINS

Stilton, a creamy-textured cow's-milk cheese, is made from a traditional recipe that creates a gentle-flavored, greenish mold. Celeriac, also known as celery root, has a pleasantly sweet smell and tastes very similar to celery. It is a versatile vegetable that in France is often eaten raw, cut into thin strips and tossed in mustard-flavored mayonnaise. It can also be boiled, then mashed into a puree. I like to slice it thinly and bake it with heavy cream in a gratin.

In this recipe celeriac's flavor blends well with the sweetness of the apple and the savory, rich-tasting cheese. If you can't find Stilton, try Gorgonzola or Roquefort. (If you use Roquefort, put less salt and cheese in the soup, as it is much stronger and saltier.)

I like to serve a basket of warm Apple-Sage Muffins to complement this soup. SERVES 6

4 tablespoons (1/2 stick) butter

1 large onion, coarsely chopped

1½ pounds celeriac, cut into small chunks

1 potato, Idaho or Yukon Gold, coarsely chopped

3 cloves garlic, crushed

2 apples, such as Braeburn, Empire, or Cox's Orange Pippin, peeled, cored, and quartered

8 to 9 cups Vegetable Stock (page 225) or water

Sea salt and freshly ground black pepper

3 ounces Stilton cheese, crumbled (2/3 cup)

Celery leaves, for garnish, optional

Celery seeds, for garnish, optional

1 recipe Apple-Sage Muffins (page 128)

Melt the butter in a large saucepan over medium heat. Add the onions, celeriac, potatoes, and garlic. Gently sweat the vegetables for 8 to 10 minutes, being careful not to brown them. Add the apples and enough vegetable stock to cover. Stir in a generous pinch of sea salt and pepper. Bring to a boil, reduce the heat, and simmer until the celeriac is tender, approximately 40 minutes. (To test, remove a chunk of the celeriac and press it with the back of a fork. If it crushes easily, it is ready.)

Ladle the soup, in batches, into a blender and puree until smooth. Return the soup to a clean saucepan over low heat and add the crumbled Stilton, stirring constantly until melted. Serve in warmed soup bowls with celery leaves and seeds scattered on top, if desired. Offer a basket of warm Apple-Sage Muffins on the side.

APPLE-SAGE MUFFINS MAKES 20 MINI MUFFINS

1 cup all-purpose flour

½ cup finely ground yellow cornmeal

¾ teaspoon baking powder

½ teaspoon baking soda

2 teaspoons coarsely chopped fresh sage leaves

½ teaspoon dry mustard

Small pinch cayenne pepper

5 tablespoons freshly grated Parmesan cheese

¼ teaspoon sea salt

1 large egg, lightly beaten

1 teaspoon sugar

4 tablespoons (½ stick) butter, melted and cooled

⅓ cup sour cream or crème fraîche

¼ cup milk

1 apple, peeled, cored, and grated

3 tablespoons goat cheese

Preheat the oven to 375°F. Lightly grease a mini-muffin tin (24 muffin cups).

Combine the flour, cornmeal, baking powder, baking soda, sage, mustard, cayenne, 3 tablespoons of the Parmesan cheese, and the salt in a medium-size bowl and set it aside.

Combine the egg and sugar together in a separate bowl. Slowly add the melted butter, stirring well. Then whisk in the sour cream and milk until combined. Fold in the grated apple.

Add the sour cream mixture to the cornmeal mixture, mixing gently with a rubber spatula until the batter is just combined. Stir in the goat cheese, allowing for clumps.

Divide the batter evenly among the muffin cups, and sprinkle the remaining 2 tablespoons Parmesan over the top. Bake for 18 to 20 minutes, or until the muffins are a light golden brown and a skewer inserted into the center of a muffin comes out clean. Leave the muffins in the tin to cool, then turn them out for serving.

CANNELLINI BEAN, PROSCIUTTO, AND MUSTARD GREENS SOUP

If you are able to get hold of the new season's dried beans, you will be amazed at the quality compared to old dried beans. They will cook much faster and more evenly. You may be even able to find fresh cannellini beans or cranberry beans in September and October; these do not require soaking. Dried beans require soaking in water, preferably overnight. If you are strapped for time, boil water, pour it over the beans, and allow to soak for a minimum of 2 hours.

This hearty soup keeps well for a few days, the taste improving overnight. When reheating the soup, you may need to add some water, as the soup will thicken as it sits. This recipe calls for a prosciutto hock, which is the end piece of the ham. It is usually difficult to slice and does not contain the best-quality meat. Therefore it is often sold as a whole piece that is ideal for cooking in stews, soups, stocks, and braises. SERVES 6

10 ounces dried cannellini beans (1½ cups)

1 hot chile pepper, such as Thai

5 cloves garlic, green shoot removed: 4 cloves crushed, 1 clove minced

1 carrot

2 stalks celery: 1 whole, 1 diced

1 onion

1 sprig rosemary, plus leaves from 2 sprigs

One 6-ounce prosciutto hock, or piece of slab bacon

1 tablespoon extra virgin olive oil, plus extra for drizzling

3 shallots, diced

Handful mustard greens, trimmed and cut into 1-by-2-inch strips

Sea salt and freshly ground black pepper

Soak the cannellini beans in water overnight.

Drain the beans and place them in a large saucepan (a large pan will allow enough room for the beans to double in size during cooking). Cover the beans with fresh water and add the chile, crushed garlic cloves, carrot, whole celery stalk, onion, rosemary sprig, and prosciutto hock. Bring to a boil over high heat. Skim off any scum that may appear on the surface. Then lower the heat and simmer the beans until they are tender, approximately 40 minutes. (The time will vary according to the age of the beans.) Every so often, give the beans a stir to ensure that they cook evenly.

Drain the beans, reserving the cooking liquid and beans separately. Discard the chile, carrot, celery stalk, rosemary sprig, and onion. Once the prosciutto hock is cool enough to handle, cut off the excess fat and then slice the meat into small bite-size strips or cubes. Set aside.

Heat the olive oil in a large saucepan over medium heat. Add the diced celery and sauté until tender, 10 to 15 minutes. Add the rosemary leaves, shallots, and minced garlic and continue to sauté for another 5 minutes. Then stir in the mustard greens, the reserved prosciutto, and salt and pepper to taste. Sauté for another minute or two. Add the beans and the reserved cooking liquid (approximately 3 cups). Stir well and simmer for 10 minutes.

Ladle approximately one third of the soup into a blender and puree. Return the puree to the soup, stirring until combined.

Serve in warmed soup bowls, with a drizzle of olive oil over each serving.

SPICED PARSNIP SOUP WITH CRUNCHY PARSNIP CHIPS

Parsnips, with their sweet, perfumed, carrot-like essence, can be used in a variety of ways. They are fantastic roasted with honey and served with duck, chicken, or beef. Or try boiling them and then mashing them with butter and grated nutmeg. Replace carrots with parsnips in a carrot cake recipe; you will be amazed how good it tastes. Parsnips are also used in Moroccan tagines, where their sweetness blends well with the warm spices, like those in this soup.

Look for firm parsnips without damp spots. A parsnip will turn spongy if stored too long. Don't worry if you don't have all of the spices listed below; make the soup with whatever you have—it will still be good. SERVES 6

1 tablespoon extra virgin olive oil

2 tablespoons butter

2 cloves garlic, crushed

1 bunch cilantro

½ hot chile pepper, such as Thai

⅛ teaspoon ground nutmeg

¼ teaspoon ground cloves

1½ teaspoons ground coriander

½ teaspoon ground cinnamon

1 teaspoon ground ginger

2 teaspoons ground cumin

¼ teaspoon ground cardamon

¼ teaspoon ground turmeric

1 large onion, coarsely chopped

1¾ pounds parsnips, coarsely chopped

Sea salt and freshly ground black pepper

6 cups Vegetable Stock (page 225), chicken stock, or water

GARNISH

⅓ cup crème fraîche

¼ cup fresh cilantro leaves

1 recipe Crunchy Parsnip Chips

Heat the olive oil and butter in a large saucepan over medium-low heat. Add the garlic, cilantro, chile, nutmeg, cloves, coriander, cinnamon, ginger, cumin, cardamom, and turmeric. Cook until fragrant, about 5 minutes.

Add the onions and parsnips, and stir well to coat them with the spices. Season with a good pinch of sea salt and pepper, and then cover with the stock. Raise the heat and bring to a boil. Reduce the heat and simmer until the parsnips are soft, approximately 25 minutes.

Remove the pan from the heat and ladle the contents, in batches, into a blender and puree until smooth. Push the puree through a sieve into a clean saucepan, discarding any solids. Reheat the soup gently. Serve in warmed soup bowls, garnished with a generous dollop of crème fraîche and a sprinkling of cilantro leaves. Serve the parsnip chips alongside.

CRUNCHY PARSNIP CHIPS

2 parsnips
Vegetable oil for deep-frying
Sea salt and freshly ground black pepper

Thinly slice the parsnips on a mandoline or box grater, or slice them as thinly as possible with a sharp knife. Half-fill a large, deep saucepan with vegetable oil. and heat it over medium heat until it reaches 350°F. Add the parsnips, in small batches, to the hot oil and fry until crisp and golden, 1 to 2 minutes. Remove them from the oil with a slotted spoon and drain on paper towels.

Season the chips liberally with sea salt and pepper and serve. They will keep well if put in an airtight container.

SPICY MUSSEL AND TOMATO SOUP

Mussels are generally sold in net bags or sacks, usually a couple of pounds per bag. Before you purchase them, take a quick look to make sure that the mussels are tightly closed. When you get home, open the bag and scrub the outside of the shells under cold running water, to remove any excess barnacles. If you can see the mussel beard (straggly gray matter attached to one side), pull it off. Throw away any mussel shells that have already opened, as there is a good chance they are dead.

Wild mussels taste better than farmed, as they have taken longer to grow and therefore have developed a more pronounced flavor. Do not buy mussels in their spawning season, when they have a softer texture and deteriorate much more quickly. Spawning season is in the summer for many mussels but not all, so check with your fishmonger. SERVES 6

MUSSELS

2 tablespoons extra virgin olive oil

2 shallots, coarsely chopped

2 cloves garlic, coarsely chopped

Handful parsley stems

Handful cilantro stems

2 pounds mussels, scrubbed and debearded

1 cup dry white wine

1 cup water

SOUP

1 tablespoon extra virgin olive oil

3 shallots finely diced

½ teaspoon finely diced preserved lemon (see page 71), optional

½ teaspoon minced garlic

¼ teaspoon chopped chile pepper, such as Thai

1 tablespoon small capers, coarsely chopped

1 anchovy fillet, coarsely chopped

½ cup coarsely chopped fresh parsley

½ cup coarsely chopped fresh cilantro

½ cup dry white wine

1 cup water

PREPARE THE MUSSELS:

Place a large colander in a bowl and set it aside.

Heat the olive oil in a large pot over medium heat. Add the shallots, garlic, and parsley and cilantro stems, and sweat for 5 minutes, being careful not to brown them. Raise the heat to high, add the mussels, wine, and water, and quickly cover the pot. Steam the mussels, shaking the pot to toss them in the steam, for 3 to 4 minutes.

Remove the lid and tip the contents of the pot into the colander. Discard any mussels that have not opened.

Pass the strained cooking liquid through a fine-mesh sieve into a clean saucepan, and cook over high heat until reduced to approximately 2¼ cups, 10 minutes. Set it aside.

Meanwhile, remove the mussels from their shells, discarding the shells (unless you wish to keep some for garnish). Cover and refrigerate the mussels until ready to use.

MAKE THE SOUP:

Heat the olive oil in a large saucepan over medium heat. Add the shallots and sauté until they are translucent, approximately 5 minutes. Add the preserved lemon, garlic, chile, capers, anchovy, and half the chopped parsley and cilantro. Continue to sauté for 2 to 3 minutes, mashing the anchovy into the garlic and shallots. Add the wine and cook until reduced by half, 8 minutes. Then add the reduced mussel stock, water, and tomatoes. Simmer gently until the mixture has reduced to a moderately thick consistency, 10 to 15 minutes.

Meanwhile, preheat the boiler.

Add the shelled mussels and the remaining chopped parsley and cilantro to the tomato mixture, season with salt and pepper, and simmer for 3 to 4 minutes.

Transfer approximately one fourth of the soup to a blender and puree. Pass the puree through a fine-mesh sieve into a bowl. Return the strained puree to the soup pot, stir-

One 16-ounce can plum tomatoes, coarsely chopped, with their juices, or 1 pound late-summer fresh tomatoes, blanched, peeled, and coarsely chopped

Sea salt and freshly ground black pepper

6 slices country bread

½ clove garlic

Extra virgin olive oil

ring well to combine. If the soup seems too thick, add vegetable stock or water to thin it to your preference. Taste the soup and adjust the seasoning if necessary.

Rub the slices of bread with the garlic clove and drizzle with olive oil. Place under the broiler until toasted on both sides. Serve with the soup.

PROSCIUTTO, WALNUT, AND GOAT CHEESE SALAD

The flavors in this salad range from salty to sweet and the textures from soft to crunchy. The salad takes little time to prepare, making it perfect to serve for a midweek supper or as an appetizer for a dinner party.

Select a variety of black grapes at the farmers' market or in your local supermarket. Look for black Muscat, Concord, or Red Flame Tokays. These old grape varieties burst with highly aromatic juices that really awaken the taste buds.

Buy the prosciutto from a reputable store that specializes in charcuterie. Ask for a sample taste and request that it be sliced thin. Don't let the fat be trimmed too much, as this is where most of the flavor is.

Look for fresh, or wet, walnuts. It is surprisingly quite easy to crack them open, and the results are definitely worth it.

The idea for the dressing for this salad was given to me by one of my past chefs, Ed Witt. Hope you enjoy it as much as we do. SERVES 6

1 tablespoon Champagne vinegar or other good-quality white wine vinegar

1 tablespoon balsamic vinegar

Smidgeon Dijon mustard

Smidgeon minced garlic

½ vanilla bean, split, seeds scraped out and reserved

Grated zest of 1 orange

1 tablespoon orange juice

2 tablespoons walnut oil

3 tablespoons extra virgin olive oil

Sea salt and freshly ground black pepper

24 walnut halves

¾ pound goat cheese, sliced into twelve ¼-inch-thick rounds

6 small handfuls peppery salad greens, such as baby red mustard or watercress

24 black grapes, halved and seeded

12 slices prosciutto

Preheat the oven to 370°F. Line a baking sheet with parchment paper.

Combine the two vinegars in a mixing bowl. Add the mustard, garlic, vanilla bean and seeds, orange zest, and orange juice. Stir well to combine. Then slowly whisk in the walnut oil and the olive oil. Season with sea salt and pepper to taste. Set the dressing aside.

Place the walnuts on another baking sheet and bake until golden brown and toasted, 6 to 8 minutes. Remove from the oven and allow to cool.

When ready to serve, place the goat cheese rounds on the prepared baking sheet and bake for 1 to 2 minutes to warm.

While the cheese is warming, toss the salad greens in a mixing bowl with a spoonful of the dressing (you may want to remove the vanilla pod to make it easier to stir the dressing) and sea salt and pepper to taste.

Layer the greens with the grapes, walnuts, warmed goat cheese, and prosciutto on six plates. Drizzle additional dressing over and around the salad. Serve immediately.

ROASTED DUCK BREAST WITH
RED MUSTARD LEAF AND FIG SALAD

For this recipe I am using the fuller-flavored duck breast, also known as duck magret, from the moulard duck. If you are looking for less of a "duck flavor," try the Pekin duck, also known as the Long Island duck.

At this time of the year you should be able to find both red and green mustard leaves at your local farmers' market. If you can't find mustard leaves, use another peppery leaf such as watercress.

If possible, try to use both black and green figs. Gently press them before purchasing to make sure they are ripe, soft, and juicy. SERVES 6

6 duck breasts

Sea salt and freshly ground black pepper

1 teaspoon light brown sugar

Grated zest and juice of 1 orange

1 tablespoon fig balsamic vinegar or regular aged balsamic vinegar

1 tablespoon sherry vinegar

2 tablespoons walnut oil

3 tablespoons extra virgin olive oil

Smidgeon minced garlic

9 ripe figs

6 slices pancetta

5 ounces duck or chicken liver, trimmed and cut into 6 equal pieces

6 fresh sage leaves, plus 1 tablespoon coarsely chopped

Six 1-inch cubes stale bread

12 cipolline onions

3 red onions, sliced into ¼-inch-thick rings

12 scallions, white part and 3 inches of green

2 sprigs thyme

1 tablespoon duck fat or vegetable oil

6 small handfuls red or green mustard leaves

Preheat the oven to 375°F.

Using a sharp knife, score a crisscross pattern on the fat side of the duck breasts. Season the duck liberally with sea salt and pepper, and set aside to come to room temperature.

Meanwhile, prepare the dressing: In a medium-size bowl, mix the brown sugar with the orange zest, orange juice, fig balsamic vinegar, sherry vinegar, walnut oil, 2 tablespoons of the olive oil, and the garlic. Slice the figs in half lengthwise and add them to the dressing. Set aside.

Lay a slice of pancetta on a clean cutting board, place a piece of duck liver in the middle, and season with a pinch of sea salt and pepper. Place a sage leaf on top of that and then a bread crouton. Wrap the crouton, encasing the liver, with the flaps of pancetta and secure with a toothpick. Repeat until you have 6 croutons. Refrigerate covered until ready to use.

Place the cipolline onions, red onions, and scallions in a bowl and add the remaining tablespoon olive oil. Add the chopped sage, thyme sprigs, and sea salt and pepper to taste. Toss to mix.

Put the cipolline and red onions in a roasting pan and roast in the oven for approximately 10 minutes. Add the scallions and continue to roast until all the onions are tender and golden brown, another 20 minutes or so. Ten minutes before the onions are done, remove the figs from the dressing with a slotted spoon, and place them alongside the onions to roast and soften. Reserve the dressing. Set the roasted onion mixture aside.

When cooking a duck breast, the goal is to achieve crisp, golden skin with the meat cooked just medium-rare. This is done by first rendering the fat from the skin, then cooking it until crisp, and finally turning the breast over to finish the cooking. So heat a sauté pan (or two if necessary) over medium-high heat. Melt the duck fat in the pan and add the duck breasts, skin side down. Cook the duck, allowing it to slowly rid itself of the excess fat, which can take up to 10 minutes (be patient). When the fat side is crisp,

pour out the excess fat and turn the breasts over. (Save the fat; it is great to have a store of it in the refrigerator for dishes such as roast potatoes.) Cook the breasts, skin side up, for approximately 3 minutes. (To test, press the middle of the breast with your finger; if it springs back quite easily, it is medium-rare. The firmer the meat, the more it is cooked.)

Transfer the duck breasts to a cutting board and set aside for at least 5 minutes.

Pour off all but 1 tablespoon of the fat from the sauté pan and add the croutons. Cook for 1 to 2 minutes on each side, until the pancetta is golden brown and crisp. Remove the croutons from the pan and keep warm.

Divide the mustard leaves, roasted onions, and figs among six plates. Slice the duck breasts and layer them over the top. Warm the reserved dressing in a saucepan and spoon it over the salads. Finish with a crouton on top of each plate.

MUSHROOM AND PARMESAN SALAD
WITH LEMON-CHIVE DRESSING

This is a very easy salad to make. Both the mushrooms and the dressing can be prepared hours in advance, covered and refrigerated, and then the salad quickly assembled at the last minute. Allow the dressing to come to room temperature before serving.

My favorite mushroom for this recipe is the porcini, or cèpe, mushroom, a wild mushroom that appears in the early autumn. Other choices are cultivated chestnut, or cremini, mushrooms, white button mushrooms, shiitakes, or oyster mushrooms. Just be sure that the mushrooms you purchase are clean, dry, firm, and unblemished.

This recipe calls for marinating raw mushrooms in lemon juice—a technique similar to a ceviche, where the acid has the effect of cooking the raw meat or fish. SERVES 6

3 tablespoons lemon juice

¼ teaspoon Dijon mustard

5 tablespoons extra virgin olive oil

Sea salt and freshly ground black pepper

1 tablespoon snipped fresh chives (¼-inch pieces)

6 ounces porcini mushrooms, sliced paper-thin

6 small handfuls salad greens, such as arugula, frisée, or watercress

6 ounces Parmesan cheese shavings (about 16 pieces)

1 tablespoon fresh marjoram leaves and/or flowers

Whisk the lemon juice with the mustard in a small bowl. Whisk in the olive oil and sea salt and pepper to taste. Stir in the chives.

Place the mushrooms in a mixing bowl and season with sea salt and pepper to taste. Toss with 3 tablespoons of the dressing. Allow to marinate for 10 minutes.

When ready to serve, layer the salad greens with the mushrooms and shaved Parmesan on six plates. Finish with a drizzle of the remaining dressing and a scattering of the marjoram leaves.

ROASTED AUTUMN VEGETABLE SALAD
WITH MAPLE-CIDER DRESSING

Try to use a wide variety of sweet, earthy autumn vegetables for this salad. When cutting them, retain their natural shape as much as possible.   SERVES 4

2 tablespoons extra virgin olive oil

2 tablespoons butter

1 tablespoon honey

1 clove garlic, minced

4 slices pumpkin, cheese pumpkin, or kabocha squash, skin on, seeds removed

4 parsnips, halved lengthwise

4 carrots, halved lengthwise

4 small sunchokes (Jerusalem artichokes; see page 178), halved

2 red onions, sliced into ¼-inch-thick rounds

2 to 3 sprigs rosemary or thyme

Sea salt and freshly ground black pepper

12 large fresh sage leaves

2 red apples, such as Braeburn, Cox's Orange Pippin, or Macoun, cored and cut into ¼-inch-thick rounds (see Note)

DRESSING

1 tablespoon cider vinegar

½ teaspoon Dijon mustard

Smidgeon minced garlic

1 teaspoon maple syrup

1 tablespoon walnut oil

2 tablespoons extra virgin olive oil

Sea salt and freshly ground black pepper

Handful arugula leaves

12 pecorino Romano shavings (shaved with a vegetable peeler), optional

Preheat the oven to 400°F.

Combine the olive oil, butter, honey, and garlic in a small saucepan and warm gently over low heat until the contents have melted together.

Place the pumpkin, parsnips, carrots, sunchokes, and onions in a large baking dish. Set aside 1 tablespoon of the honey mixture. Pour the remainder over the vegetables, and using your hands, gently toss the vegetables to coat them. Add the rosemary sprigs and season liberally with sea salt and pepper.

Roast for 15 minutes. Give the pan a gentle shake and add the sage leaves. Continue to roast until the vegetables are golden brown and tender, another 20 minutes. If some of them look as though they are ready before the others, pull them out of the pan and set aside. Remove the pan from the oven and allow the vegetables to cool to room temperature. Discard the rosemary sprigs.

Meanwhile, warm the remaining 1 tablespoon honey mixture in a saucepan over medium heat. Add the apple slices to the pan in a single layer (you may have to do this in batches). Gently sauté the apples until they are golden brown, approximately 8 minutes. Remove from the heat and allow to cool.

Prepare the dressing: Combine the cider vinegar, mustard, garlic, and maple syrup in a bowl. Whisk in the walnut oil and olive oil until combined. Season with sea salt and pepper to taste.

To serve, arrange the vegetables with the apples, arugula, and pecorino cheese, if desired, on four plates. Drizzle the dressing over and around the salad.

NOTE:
If you have a very small (½-inch) round pastry cutter, cut the apple into slices and then cut out the core with the pastry cutter.

CRAB SALAD WITH PICKLED EGGPLANT, SHAVED FENNEL, AND RADISH

I think a crab salad should be kept as simple as possible so that you can savor the sweet-tasting meat. Here I have partnered crabmeat with a few shaved vegetables and a clean-tasting eggplant pickle. This interesting eggplant recipe, adapted from Lucy Norris's wonderful book *Pickled*, is easy and adds an unusual dimension to many dishes. The recipe will make more than you require for the crab salad, but the extra will keep well in the fridge for at least a week. Try serving it with grilled tuna or mixing it with boiled shrimp for a sandwich filling.

As for the crabmeat, consider using jumbo lump crabmeat for this recipe. It is sold at a premium because only the largest chunks of meat are used. Make sure you buy a recently packed container; if there is no date on it, ask the fishmonger.

SERVES 4

3 bulbs baby fennel or 1 bulb regular fennel, outer layer removed

6 radishes (French radish or watermelon radish or a combination)

3 tablespoons lemon juice

5 tablespoons extra virgin olive oil

Sea salt and freshly ground black pepper

1 tablespoon coarsely chopped fresh chervil

1 tablespoon snipped fresh chives (¼-inch pieces)

¾ pound jumbo lump crabmeat

4 tablespoons Pickled Eggplant (see below)

1 recipe Coriander Crisp Bread (page 150)

Shave the fennel and radishes on a mandoline or box grater, or slice them as thinly as possible with a sharp knife. Place them in a small bucket of ice water until ready to use. (You can leave them as long as overnight.)

Whisk the lemon juice and olive oil together in a bowl, and season with sea salt and pepper to taste.

Remove the fennel and radishes from the ice water, pat them dry, and place them in a bowl. Add the chervil and chives. Add a couple spoonfuls of the dressing and a pinch of sea salt and pepper, and toss well. The remaining dressing can be stored in the refrigerator in a sealed container for 2 days.

To assemble the salad, layer the crabmeat, vegetables, and eggplant pickle on four plates. Serve with the flat bread.

PICKLED EGGPLANT   MAKES 1 CUP

2 eggplants (2 pounds total)

½ tablespoon toasted sesame oil

2 to 3 tablespoons chopped fresh cilantro

½ teaspoon sea salt

6 tablespoons rice vinegar

1 tablespoon sugar

2 tablespoons soy sauce

1 tablespoon grated fresh ginger

½ tablespoon grated garlic

½ teaspoon chopped hot chile pepper, such as Thai

Bring about 2 inches of water to a boil in a saucepan. Place the whole eggplant in a colander and sit the colander over the simmering water. Place a lid over the top, and steam until the eggplant is completely cooked, 20 minutes. Then remove the colander from the simmering water and let the eggplant sit in the colander until it is cool.

Peel the eggplant and coarsely chop the flesh. Combine all the remaining ingredients in a bowl. Add the eggplant and toss together. Cover and chill in the refrigerator for at least 2 hours or up to 3 to 4 days before serving.

CORIANDER CRISP BREAD   MAKES ABOUT 12 PIECES

2 cups all-purpose flour

¼ teaspoon baking powder

½ teaspoon salt

4 tablespoons plus 1 teaspoon butter, softened

½ cup plus 1 tablespoon buttermilk

1 teaspoon coriander seeds, coarsely crushed

Whisk the flour, baking powder, and salt together in a large bowl. Rub the butter into the flour until it resembles coarse meal. Add the buttermilk and combine until it forms a dough (don't worry if it is sticky). Let the dough rest in the bowl in the refrigerator, covered, for 1 hour.

Preheat the oven to 325°F. Line two baking sheets with parchment paper.

Divide the dough into quarters and roll each into a long strip approximately 1/16 inch thick. These do not have to be precise shapes or sizes. Place the strips of dough on the prepared baking sheets and sprinkle with the coriander seeds. Bake until golden brown, approximately 6 minutes. Remove from the oven and allow to cool on wire racks. Break the flat bread into individual pieces for serving. Store the bread in an airtight container for up to 2 days.

POMEGRANATE-GLAZED QUAIL
WITH CINNAMON-RAISIN TABBOULEH

The small, intricate carcass of the quail can be tricky to eat and is best tackled with your hands. (If you prefer to debone the quail, ask your butcher to "tunnel"-bone them—the carcass is removed without cutting into the flesh, leaving the wing tips and legs.) I prefer to cook quail with all bones intact, as it helps retain the flavor. And I don't mind getting my fingers sticky!

Tabbouleh is a Middle Eastern dish made with bulgur wheat that is marinated with lemon juice, chopped fresh herbs, and olive oil. There are many variations, utilizing an array of spices and herbs. The important thing to remember is to season it generously. Making the tabbouleh ahead of time allows the wheat to soak up even more flavor from the marinade.

The glaze for the quail requires pomegranate molasses. This treacle-thick brown sauce with its tart flavor can be found in speciality food shops. SERVES 2

TABBOULEH

½ to ¾ cup chicken stock or water

Pinch ground cinnamon

½ teaspoon ground cumin

¼ teaspoon sweet paprika

Pinch cayenne pepper

1 clove garlic, minced

2 shallots, finely diced

¼ teaspoon sea salt

1 cup bulgur wheat

2 tablespoons extra virgin olive oil

2 to 3 tablespoons lemon juice

Grated zest of 1 lemon

Seeds of ½ pomegranate

3 tablespoons unsalted pistachio nuts, coarsely chopped

Small handful golden raisins

½ cup chopped fresh flat-leaf parsley

½ cup chopped fresh mint

½ cup chopped fresh cilantro

Juice of 1 lime

3 tablespoons pomegranate molasses

1 teaspoon orange-flower water, optional

½ teaspoon ground cumin

Prepare the tabbouleh: Bring about 2 inches of water to a simmer in a saucepan. Pour the chicken stock into another saucepan and add the cinnamon, cumin, paprika, cayenne, garlic, shallots, and salt. Bring to a boil. Place the bulgur in a heatproof bowl and add the boiling stock mixture, stirring well. Cover the bowl with a plate or lid of some sort, and then set the bowl over the saucepan of simmering water. Steam, stirring every so often, until the wheat has absorbed the stock and is tender and plump, approximately 20 minutes. Remove the bowl from the heat and stir in the olive oil, lemon juice, lemon zest, all but 1 tablespoon of the pomegranate seeds, and the pistachios and raisins. Taste and adjust the seasoning if necessary. When the tabbouleh has cooled completely, add the chopped parsley, mint, and cilantro. (If the tabbouleh sits for any length of time, it will absorb the juices and will perhaps need an extra slug of olive oil or lemon juice before serving.)

Preheat the oven to 375°F.

Place the lime juice, pomegranate molasses, orange-flower water, cumin, cinnamon, and brown sugar in a heavy-bottomed saucepan and simmer over medium heat until the mixture has reduced to a sticky glaze, approximately 10 minutes.

Brush the quail with the glaze and place them in a roasting pan. Roast for 15 to 20 minutes, every so often brushing a little more glaze over the quail. The quail skin will be golden brown and crisp. To test for doneness, insert a skewer into the thickest part of the leg. The juices should run clear.

Place the tabbouleh on a serving dish and arrange the quail on top. Garnish with the watercress and scatter the reserved pomegranate seeds over the quail. Serve with the Yogurt Dressing on the side, if desired.

¼ teaspoon ground cinnamon

1 tablespoon light brown sugar

6 quail, cleaned, deboned if desired

1 large bunch watercress or arugula, trimmed

1 recipe Yogurt Dressing (page 85), optional

WARM PROSCIUTTO, MUSHROOM, TALEGGIO, AND SPINACH SANDWICH

Taleggio, a rich, soft, Italian cow's-milk cheese, has a very strong smell, especially when heated. It pairs wonderfully with the sweet and salty prosciutto in this sandwich. If you prefer to use another variety of cheese, try mozzarella or Gorgonzola.
MAKES 1 SANDWICH

5 tablespoons extra virgin olive oil

Generous handful baby spinach, leaves trimmed

Smidgeon minced garlic

Sea salt and freshly ground black pepper

Small handful mushrooms, sliced

2 slices country-style bread

2 slices prosciutto

2 slices Taleggio cheese

Heat 1 tablespoon of the olive oil in a sauté pan over medium heat. Add the spinach, garlic, and sea salt and pepper to taste. Sauté for 1 to 2 minutes. As soon as the spinach has wilted, drain it in a colander or sieve, pressing on it with a spoon to remove as much liquid as possible.

Add 2 tablespoons of the olive oil to the same pan and place over medium-high heat. Add the mushrooms and sea salt and pepper to taste. Sauté until the mushrooms are golden brown, approximately 10 minutes. Remove the mushrooms from the pan and set them aside.

To assemble the sandwich, place the bread on a cutting board and layer the spinach, prosciutto, mushrooms, and Taleggio on top. Cover with the second piece of bread.

Warm the remaining 2 tablespoons olive oil in a sauté pan over medium heat and add the sandwich. Sauté gently until the bread is golden brown, 3 to 4 minutes. Then, using a spatula, carefully flip the sandwich over to brown the other side. Continue to sauté until the cheese has started to melt and the filling is hot, 3 to 4 minutes more. Serve immediately.

LANCASHIRE CHEESE

The cheese sandwich that follows is really an excuse to tell you about Mrs. Kirkham, who makes a fantastic cheese. England's Lancashire county is famous for the its tangy, creamy cow's-milk cheese. Mrs. Kirkham has been making this cheese for the past 30 years, 365 days a year. She is the third generation in her family to make Lancashire following the traditional method—combining half of the milk from each day with the milk from the next day. The unpasteurized milk, from the farm's dairy cows (Mrs. Kirkham is on first-name terms with them all), can vary from day to day according to the weather, the season, and the cows. She skillfully adapts the craft of making the cheese to these variables.

Now, I am not saying you have to search high and low to find Lancashire cheese. What I am saying is, stop and think about how cheese is produced. The next time you are in the supermarket, poke your nose around the varieties offered. Ask the cheese purveyor where the cheeses are from. Are they unpasteurized? Are they from a small production? Are they free of artificial colorings? If you are able to find locally produced cheese, ask to taste it. Mrs. Kirkham claims to have tasted every single batch of cheese she has made, ensuring it has reached optimum flavor and is in prime condition. You can't get more devotion and care than this. The more love poured into the production, the more rewarding the taste. It speaks for itself, really.

LANCASHIRE CHEESE SANDWICH WITH FIG CHUTNEY

I don't need to tell you how to make a cheese sandwich, but I would like to suggest that you make the fig chutney and pair it with some Lancashire cheese.

FIG CHUTNEY MAKES APPROXIMATELY 1 QUART

This chutney is a treat to have in your refrigerator. It's good with a variety of cheeses and cold meats. Try spreading it on bruschetta with warm goat cheese or serving it with baked ham. Plan ahead when making this recipe, as the results are better if the figs are marinated overnight.

1½ pounds ripe black or green figs

½ cup red wine vinegar

1 hot chile pepper, such as Thai, seeded and cut into thin strips

2 tablespoons light brown sugar

Grated zest and juice of 1 orange

One 2-inch piece cinnamon stick

1 tablespoon vegetable oil

1 onion, finely diced

1 clove garlic, minced

1 tablespoon grated fresh ginger

1 teaspoon cumin seeds, coarsely crushed

1 teaspoon coriander seeds, coarsely crushed

1 teaspoon yellow mustard seeds

¼ teaspoon sea salt

⅛ teaspoon ground cloves

1 cup water

Place the figs, vinegar, chile strips, brown sugar, orange zest and juice, and cinnamon stick in a bowl; stir well to combine. Cover with plastic wrap and place in the refrigerator for at least 4 hours or, preferably, overnight.

Heat the vegetable oil in a good-size saucepan over medium heat. Add the onions, garlic, ginger, cumin, coriander, mustard seeds, salt, and cloves. Sweat, stirring with a wooden spoon, for 5 minutes, making sure the onions do not brown. Add the marinated figs and the water, and stir well. Reduce the heat and cook, stirring frequently, until the chutney is thick, about 40 minutes.

Let the chutney cool completely. Then spoon it into sterilized glass jars. It will keep for a couple of months in the refrigerator.

GORGONZOLA, PEAR, AND HONEY
OPEN-FACED SANDWICH

Gorgonzola is a creamy Italian cow's-milk cheese with greenish veins. Its pleasantly sharp flavor is very well matched with pears. A drizzle of honey adds an extra sweet dimension. Choose an interesting-flavored honey, such as wildflower or chestnut. Eat this sandwich on its own as a snack, or serve it as a cheese course. MAKES 2 SANDWICHES

2 slices walnut bread

2 slices Gorgonzola cheese

1 ripe pear (Comice, Seckel, or Bartlett), peeled, quartered, and cored

1 teaspoon honey

Small bunch watercress, trimmed

Toast the walnut bread. Place the Gorgonzola slices on top of the hot toast. Slice the quartered pear into thin wedges and arrange them over the Gorgonzola. Drizzle a very thin trickle of honey over the cheese and pear in zigzag fashion. Serve immediately, garnished with watercress on the side.

FRANK SORBELLO

Frank Sorbello is a farmer in New York's Hudson Valley. The farm, a dried-up river bed that has been in the Sorbello family since the 1920s, is prized for its naturally irrigated and nutrient-rich black soil. This can have its downside. Every time there are heavy rains, the farm drowns and Frank loses not only his crops, but also his livelihood. The natural spring that runs through the land is ideal for growing watercress. Frank gets a crop in the spring and then a second crop in the autumn.

RICOTTA, FIG, AND PISTACHIO PANETTONE

Panettone is northern Italy's traditional Christmas cake. This unusually large, dome-shaped bread is flavored with warm spices and orange and lemon peel. You will see panettone displayed in brightly colored boxes hanging from the ceiling of Italian delicatessens. I like to use panettone in a variety of dessert bread recipes, such as bread and butter pudding.

The recipe makes more than enough poaching liquid. Store the extra in the refrigerator—it will keep for at least 1 month—and use it to poach other seasonal fruits, such as pears, quince, plums, and dates.

If you don't have time to make the poaching liquid, it's not a problem. Just slice the figs, drizzle them with a little orange juice, and arrange them over the ricotta-topped panettone. SERVES 2

POACHING LIQUID

2 cups sweet white wine

¾ cup port

1½ cups sugar

1 vanilla bean, split lengthwise

3 strips orange peel

Juice of 1 orange

One 2-inch cinnamon stick

2 whole cloves

Pinch freshly grated nutmeg

5 black peppercorns, crushed

2 cups water

6 ripe black or green figs

½ cup ricotta cheese

1 tablespoon slivered unsalted pistachio nuts

Grated zest of 1 orange

1 tablespoon or small chunk dark chocolate, cut into small pieces

2 slices panettone

Confectioners' sugar, for dusting

Prepare the poaching liquid: Pour the wine and port into a heavy-bottomed saucepan, and add the sugar, vanilla bean, orange peel and juice, cinnamon stick, cloves, nutmeg, peppercorns, and water. Simmer over moderate heat for 30 minutes. Strain 3 cups of the liquid into a clean saucepan. Strain the remaining liquid into a container and store in the refrigerator for another use.

Add the figs to the poaching liquid in the saucepan, completely immersing them. Place a small plate or lid on top of the figs to help keep them submerged. Simmer gently for 10 minutes, or until the figs are soft to the touch.

While the figs are poaching, mix the ricotta, pistachios, orange zest, and chocolate pieces together in a bowl.

Remove the figs with a slotted spoon and set them aside. Bring the liquid to a boil and cook until it has the consistency of a syrup, about 10 minutes. Then pass the syrup through a strainer into a pitcher and set it aside.

Toast the panettone. Spread the ricotta mixture over the toast. Slice the figs in half and arrange them over the ricotta. Drizzle some of the poaching syrup over the top, dust with confectioners' sugar, and serve.

SAUSAGE, MUSHROOM, AND
MELTED CHEESE SANDWICHES

The mushrooms and melted cheese in this sandwich make for a savory and comforting meal. MAKES 2 SANDWICHES

2 good-quality chicken, veal, or beef
　sausages (see page 167)

1 strip bacon, cut into small strips

2 tablespoons butter or duck fat

1 shallot, finely diced

5 ounces assorted mushrooms, such
　as chanterelles, girolles, porcini,
　cremini, and/or button, sliced

2 tablespoons crème fraîche

Sea salt and freshly ground black
　pepper

2 tablespoons grated strong, hard
　cheese, such as farmhouse
　Cheddar

½ tablespoon coarsely chopped
　fresh parsley or chives

Dijon mustard

2 rolls or individual baguettes

Preheat the oven to 375°F.

Place the sausages in an ovenproof dish and bake until cooked through, about 10 minutes. (They will be firm to the touch when cooked.)

Meanwhile, cook the bacon in a sauté pan over medium heat until the fat has rendered and the bacon is crisp. Remove the bacon from the pan with a slotted spoon and set it aside. Melt the butter in the same pan, add the shallots and mushrooms, and sauté until golden brown, approximately 10 minutes.

Return the bacon to the pan, lower the heat, and add the crème fraîche and a pinch of sea salt and pepper. Simmer for 1 minute. Then scatter the cheese over the mushrooms and cover the pan. When the cheese has melted, remove the lid and sprinkle the parsley over the top.

Smear the mustard inside the rolls and add the sausages. Serve immediately with a generous dollop of mushrooms, bacon, and melted cheese on top.

HOMEMADE SAUSAGE

TRY MAKING THESE EASY SAUSAGES AT HOME: Take a pound of ground pork, beef, lamb, or other meat and mix it with a finely chopped onion, a chopped garlic clove, a pinch of sea salt and pepper, and a beaten egg. Add a variety of seasonings to this:

- *Ground pork goes well with crushed fennel seeds, chopped sage, and lemon zest.*
- *Ground beef goes well with chopped thyme, grated horseradish, and Worcestershire sauce.*
- *Ground lamb goes well with orange zest, chopped chile, and ground cumin.*

Using your hands, shape the meat into sausage shapes. Cook as you would any other sausage.

SMOKED SALMON AND SCRAMBLED EGG BAGEL

There is a wide variety of smoked salmon to choose from. I prefer using Scottish smoked salmon; it's rich and fatty, but not oily, and has a wonderful complex flavor. If you are prepared to slice the salmon yourself, it is the best option. Buy a whole side and slice it with a long flexible knife as needed. The salmon will keep well in the refrigerator for at least 2 weeks. If you are using presliced smoked salmon, look on the labeling to make sure it's without added colorings and preservatives.
SERVES 2

4 slices smoked salmon

5 large eggs

Sea salt and freshly ground black
   pepper

1 tablespoon butter

2 tablespoons heavy cream

2 bagels, cut in half horizontally

Watercress, for garnish

½ red onion, thinly sliced

1 teaspoon capers

1 tablespoon fresh flat-leaf parsley
   leaves

Remove the smoked salmon from the refrigerator at least 20 minutes ahead to bring it to room temperature.

Crack the eggs into a mixing bowl, and whisk lightly with a pinch of sea salt and pepper. Melt the butter in a saucepan over medium heat. Add the eggs and stir with a wooden spoon until they have started to thicken and set, approximately 4 minutes. Remove the eggs from the heat and stir in the heavy cream. Set aside.

Toast the bagels. Spoon the scrambled eggs over each bagel half and arrange the smoked salmon on top. Garnish with the watercress. Serve the onions, capers, and parsley on the side.

WINTER

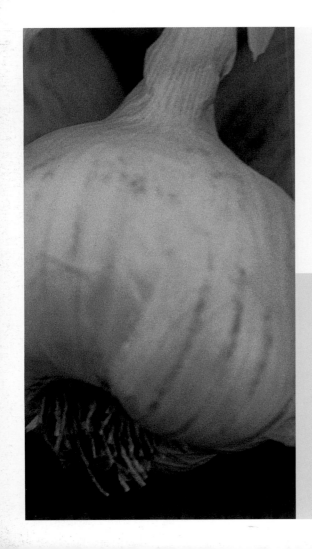

SOUPS

Sausage, Potato, and Kale Soup

Jerusalem Artichoke Soup

Curried Lentil, Sweet Potato, and Bacon Soup

Fish Soup with Aioli

Onion, White Bean, and Gruyère Soup

Chilled Mango Soup with Sesame-Lime Cookies

SALADS

Good Caesar Salad

Persimmon, Date, and Pecorino Salad

Squid with Chile-Lime Black Bean Salad

Grapefruit, Blue Cheese, and Celery Salad

Confit Duck, Fennel, Blood Orange,
and Watercress Salad

Citrus and Endive Salad with Mint Yogurt

Shrimp, Roasted Cherry Tomato,
and Watercress Salad

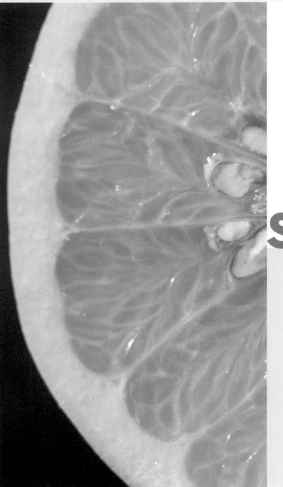

SANDWICHES

Shrimp Roll with Tomato Cocktail Relish

Smoked Salmon Club

Spicy Steak Sandwich with Chipotle Mayonnaise
and Buttermilk Fried Onion Rings

Ham and Brie Sandwich with Apple-Walnut Salad

Turkey Sandwich with Cranberry-Pear Relish

Pain Perdu with Roasted Apples

Even though this is a slow period for growing produce, there is no need to let your cooking suffer the winter blues. Comfort yourself with sweet-tasting, slow-cooked root vegetables, lentils, and dried beans. Bring salads to life with a variety of citrus fruits, from honey mandarins to blood oranges, kumquats, white and pink grapefruits, limes and clementines. Introduce a touch of the exotic with persimmons, dates, almonds, and warm spices. Seafood thrives at this time of the year, the cold water helping to maintain the firm and succulent flesh of the fish. Find time to preserve some winter goodies, such as Cranberry-Pear Relish. Experiment with making your own mustard. Make duck confit to enjoy over the winter months.

In need of a brief respite from New York's winter chill, I escaped to Florida to meet with Charlie Andrews, an organic farmer who produces an amazing array of greens, vegetables, and herbs that truly inspire the cook. I also met Robin Lauriault, whose boyhood passion for citrus fruit inspired him to plant his own citrus grove. This spectacular grove is home to thirty-six varieties of citrus fruit including Amber Sweet oranges, pineapple oranges, and tangelos. By introducing you to these farmers, I hope to encourage you to connect with the earth and think about what you are eating and where it is coming from.

HERE IS A LIST OF ITEMS FOUND IN THE WINTER:

Brussels sprouts
Cabbage
Carrots
Celery root
Citrus fruit
Cranberries
Endive
Jerusalem artichokes
Kale
Parsnips
Variety of potatoes
Rutabaga
Persimmons
Quince
Radishes
Romaine lettuce
Variety of seafood
Spinach
Treviso radicchio
Tropical fruit
Turnips
Winter squash

SAUSAGE, POTATO, AND KALE SOUP

In this soup, similar to the Portuguese *caldo verde*, highly seasoned sausage is partnered with potatoes to yield a hearty peasant-style soup, ideal for keeping the winter blues away. I like to use fresh chorizo, a spicy Spanish pork sausage seasoned with paprika for this recipe.

Potato is a great base for soups because of its affinity to blend with other ingredients. As the potato breaks down during cooking, not only does it add a wonderful thick consistency to the broth but it also soaks up all the flavors in the pot.

SERVES 4

1 tablespoon extra virgin olive oil

½ pound high-quality well-seasoned pork, beef, or lamb sausages

1 large white onion, cut into ½-inch dice

1 clove garlic, minced

¾ pound baking potatoes, cut into 1-inch pieces

1 tablespoon chopped fresh sage, rosemary, or thyme

4 cups chicken stock or Vegetable Stock (page 225)

Sea salt and freshly ground black pepper

Large handful kale, trimmed and sliced into thin strips

Heat the olive oil in a large, heavy-bottomed saucepan over medium heat. Add the sausages and cook until golden brown, approximately 2 minutes on each side. Remove the sausages from the pan and set aside. Discard all but 1 generous tablespoon of the fat remaining in the pan.

Place the pan back on the heat and add the onions. Stir well and sauté until translucent, approximately 5 minutes. Add the garlic and continue to sauté for another minute. Add the potatoes, stir well, and then add the sage and stock. Season with sea salt and pepper to taste, and bring to a boil. Then lower the heat and simmer gently for 10 minutes.

Slice the sausages into bite-size pieces and add them to the soup. Continue to simmer the soup until the potatoes are cooked through and have started to collapse, approximately 10 minutes. Add the kale and simmer for 5 to 8 minutes, until cooked through. Taste the soup and adjust the seasoning if necessary. Serve piping hot.

curly-leaf Redbor kale

CHARLIE AND THE (BUG-FREE)
GREENS FACTORY

Eighteen years and three thousand miles ago, Charlie Andrews left Silicon Valley for the fertile fields and searing heat of central Florida. Today, Charlie teases some of the country's best greens, including Castelfranco and Tango lettuce, Tuscan kale, and Romanesque (a broccoli and cauliflower cross), from the sandy soil of his five-acre organic farm.

Recognizing the difficulty restaurants have with serving customers imperfect greens, Charlie initiated the rigorous process of growing his produce in small batches and turning over varietals every month in order to minimize infestations of "gourmet" bugs. These gluttonous bugs, unlike their human counterparts, tend to spurn variety in their diets and therefore thrive when the same produce is replanted season after season. At large, industrial farms, such labor-intensive replanting is impossible, so they turn to chemicals to suppress the bug population. Charlie relies on speed and variety to get his greens to the market before the insects learn to adapt. Charlie is the H&M of vegetable suppliers!

Charlie is also an educator and invites local schools to his farm to connect with the land and its bounty. During the harsh New York winters, I always look forward to Charlie's Florida greens to brighten my menus.

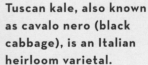

Tuscan kale, also known as cavalo nero (black cabbage), is an Italian heirloom varietal.

JERUSALEM ARTICHOKE SOUP

Jerusalem artichokes, also known as sunchokes (no relation to the globe artichoke), have a wonderfully sweet and nutty flavor. They are a very versatile vegetable that can be roasted, pureed, or shaved and eaten raw. Choose Jerusalem artichokes that are firm, with unblemished skin. When cleaning, look out for small clumps of mud hiding in the knobby crevices. Don't peel the skins, as they are full of iron—just give them a good scrub. If you are serving the artichokes raw, squeeze fresh lemon juice over them to prevent discoloration.

This elegant and creamy soup can be dressed up or down depending on the garnish. Try roasting slivers of hazelnuts or Brazil nuts and scattering them over the top, finishing with a drizzle of their respective oil. If you want something a little snazzier, crisp thinly sliced prosciutto in the oven, panfry some tiny bay scallops, and arrange both on top of the soup. And if you *really* feel like a treat, garnish the soup with shavings of black truffle.   SERVES 4

1 tablespoon olive oil

1 tablespoon butter

1 onion, finely diced

1 stalk celery, finely diced

1 clove garlic, minced

1½ pounds Jerusalem artichokes, trimmed

Sea salt and freshly ground black pepper

1 sprig thyme

4 cups chicken stock or Vegetable Stock (page 225)

⅓ cup heavy cream

Heat the olive oil and butter in a heavy-bottomed saucepan over medium heat. Add the onions, celery, garlic, and Jerusalem artichokes, and sweat the vegetables for 5 minutes, stirring them now and again with a wooden spoon and being careful not to brown them. Season with sea salt and pepper to taste, and add the thyme sprig.

Pour the stock into the pan and bring to a boil. Stir, lower the heat, and simmer until the vegetables are tender, approximately 25 minutes.

Remove the pan from the heat and discard the thyme sprig. Working in batches, ladle the soup into a blender and puree. Pass the puree through a fine-mesh strainer into a clean saucepan, pressing on it with a spoon. Add the heavy cream and reheat gently, stirring until the cream is thoroughly combined and the soup is hot. Serve immediately.

CURRIED LENTIL, SWEET POTATO, AND BACON SOUP

Use either green or brown lentils for this soup—they cook in more or less the same amount of time. You could also use red lentils, adding them 10 minutes after you have added the stock. If you don't have curry powder, make your own concoction with ground cumin, coriander, turmeric, cardamom, and cayenne pepper. SERVES 6

1 tablespoon olive oil

3 strips thick-sliced bacon, cut into ½-inch pieces

1 large onion, finely diced

1 stalk celery, finely diced

1 small leek (white part only), finely diced

1 clove garlic, minced

1 large sweet potato, cut into ½-inch cubes

1 cup green or brown lentils

1 to 2 teaspoons curry powder, to taste

1 tablespoon chopped fresh sage, optional

1 tablespoon chopped fresh thyme, optional

9 cups chicken stock or Vegetable Stock (page 225)

Sea salt and freshly ground black pepper

½ cup coarsely chopped fresh flat-leaf parsley

½ cup coarsely chopped fresh cilantro

Heat the olive oil in a large, heavy-bottomed saucepan over medium heat. Add the bacon and sauté until it is brown and crisp, 6 to 8 minutes. Remove the bacon with a slotted spoon and set it aside on paper towels.

Add the onions and celery to the pan and sauté gently for 10 minutes. If the pan gets too hot, add a splash of the stock and stir well.

Add the leeks, garlic, sweet potatoes, lentils, curry powder, and the sage and thyme, if desired. Sauté for another 5 minutes. Return the bacon to the pan and add the stock. Season with sea salt and pepper to taste, and bring to a boil. Then reduce the heat and simmer until the vegetables and lentils are tender, approximately 30 minutes.

Add the parsley and cilantro, stir well, and serve.

FISH SOUP WITH AIOLI

Every country has its regional variations on fish soup. I particularly like this recipe because, even though there is a long list of ingredients, it is easy to put together. You can make the stock and marinate the fish ahead of time. Then, at the last moment, all you have to do is cook the fish in the stock. This makes it ideal for entertaining.

A flavorful fish stock is essential. Ask your fishmonger to include the bones when you buy the fish fillets. Use these, plus the shrimp shells and the trimmings from the fillets, to make the stock. Use as few or as many different types of fish as you like, following this recipe as a guide.

Serve the soup in its cooking vessel or in a large tureen at the table for guests to help themselves. The accompanying aioli is essential to the flavor and consistency. Make sure you encourage your guests to swirl copious amounts of it into the broth. Serve hot crusty bread on the side. SERVES 4

FISH STOCK

6 cups water

1 cup dry white wine

1 onion, finely sliced

1 stalk celery, finely sliced

1½ pounds fish bones, trimmings and head from white-fleshed fish (cut into 2- to 3-inch pieces), and shrimp shells

Small handful parsley sprigs

6 black or white peppercorns

2 bay leaves

SOUP

1 pound boneless, firm-fleshed fish fillets, such as snapper, halibut, red mullet, cod, or monkfish

12 shrimp, shelled

2 medium squid, cleaned (see page 195), cut into bite-size pieces and scored in a crisscross pattern

3 tablespoons olive oil

Grated zest of 1 lemon

3 cloves garlic, green shoot removed: 1 clove minced, 2 cloves sliced paper-thin

½ teaspoon finely chopped hot chile pepper, such as Thai

Prepare the stock: Place all the stock ingredients in a large saucepan and bring to a boil over high heat. Skim off any scum that appears on the surface, lower the heat, and simmer for 20 minutes. Strain the stock through a fine-mesh sieve into a large measuring cup and discard the solids. The stock can be prepared a day in advance, covered, and refrigerated.

Marinate the fish: Cut the fish fillets into large bite-size pieces and place them in a small bowl. Place the shrimp and squid in a separate bowl. Add ½ tablespoon of the olive oil to each bowl, and divide the lemon zest, minced garlic, chile, parsley, chives, and fennel fronds between them. Stir well to coat the seafood evenly, and cover with plastic wrap. Place both bowls in the refrigerator for at least 1 hour and up to 6.

Heat the remaining 2 tablespoons olive oil in a saucepan over medium heat. Add the onions, fennel, and sliced garlic, and sweat for 8 to 10 minutes, being careful not to brown them. Add the tomatoes and 3 cups of the fish stock, and bring to a boil. Then lower the heat and simmer gently for 8 to 10 minutes.

Add the marinated fish fillets to the soup and simmer for 2 to 3 minutes. Add the clams and mussels, cover the pan, and cook, shaking the pan occasionally, for 2 to 3 minutes. Remove the lid and add the marinated shrimp and squid. Simmer until the shells have opened and all of the fish is cooked, about 1 minute. Discard any shells that haven't opened.

Serve immediately, with the Aioli and toasted country bread alongside.

1 tablespoon coarsely chopped fresh
   flat-leaf parsley

1 tablespoon coarsely chopped fresh
   chives

1 tablespoon coarsely chopped fennel
   fronds

1 onion, halved and sliced

½ bulb (about ¼ pound) fennel,
   tough outer layer removed, sliced

1 cup canned plum tomatoes, drained
   and coarsely chopped

Small handful littleneck or Manila
   clams, washed under cold running
   water

Small handful mussels, cleaned under
   cold running water

1 recipe Aioli (page 24)

Sliced country bread, such as
   sourdough or pugliese, toasted

ONION, WHITE BEAN, AND GRUYÈRE SOUP

Unlike the traditional brown French onion soup, where the sliced onions are caramelized and braised in a meaty broth, this onion soup is a sweet, white, creamy puree. I have added the beans whole for texture. You can cheat and use canned beans, but make sure you rinse them well; substitute vegetable stock for the bean-cooking liquid.

Gruyère is a distinctly strong, nutty-flavored, cow's-milk cheese from Switzerland that melts easily, making it perfect for this soup. SERVES 4

BEANS

¾ cup dried cannellini or butter
  beans

½ onion

2 cloves garlic, crushed

1 stalk celery

2 bay leaves

2 sprigs sage

1 teaspoon sea salt

2 tablespoons butter

2 pounds onions, coarsely sliced

Sea salt and freshly ground black
  pepper

3 ounces Gruyère cheese, grated
  (1 cup)

1 teaspoon fresh thyme leaves

1 baguette, sliced and toasted

Soak the beans in water overnight.

Drain the beans and place them in a large saucepan (allowing enough room for the beans to double in size during cooking). Cover with plenty of water. Add the onion half, garlic, celery, bay leaves, and sage. Bring to a boil and skim off any foam that appears on the surface. Lower the heat and simmer for 30 minutes. Then add the sea salt and continue to simmer until the beans are tender, about 10 more minutes. (The time will vary according to the age and variety of bean.) Drain the beans, reserving the cooking liquid and beans separately. Discard the vegetables and herbs.

Heat the butter in a saucepan over medium heat. Add the sliced onions and season with salt and pepper to taste. Sweat the onions until they are soft and translucent, about 15 minutes. Add 4 cups of the reserved bean-cooking liquid and bring to a boil. Then lower the heat and simmer until the onions are cooked, approximately 25 minutes.

Ladle the soup, in batches, into a blender and puree. Return the soup to a clean saucepan and add the beans, Gruyère, and thyme leaves. Heat until the soup is hot and the cheese has melted. Serve with the toasted baguette.

CHILLED MANGO SOUP WITH SESAME-LIME COOKIES

My favorite mangoes are the highly aromatic yellow-skinned ones from India. This is one fruit that benefits from being exported underripe, as they ripen successfully after picking.

This exotic aromatic soup is ideal for cleansing the palate and is great served as a pre-dessert course. SERVES 4

1 teaspoon coriander seeds

6 cardamom pods

½ teaspoon pink peppercorns, plus a few extra for garnish

¼ teaspoon black peppercorns

½ teaspoon ground fenugreek

3 ripe mangoes, peeled

2½ cups water

1 tablespoon coarsely chopped fresh ginger (1-inch piece)

1 tablespoon coarsely chopped lemongrass (2- to 3-inch piece)

1 tablespoon sugar

Sea salt to taste

⅓ cup thick yogurt, such as Greek yogurt or thickened regular yogurt (see Note, page 97)

1 recipe Sesame-Lime Cookies (see below)

Place the coriander seeds, cardamom pods, pink and black peppercorns, and fenugreek on a chopping board and crush lightly with the side of a wide, heavy knife. Transfer the spices to a sauté pan and toast over low heat until fragrant, 2 to 3 minutes. Set aside.

Coarsely chop 2 of the mangoes and place them in a blender. Add ½ cup of the water and puree. Slice the remaining mango into thin strips and set them aside.

Put the mango puree in a saucepan and add the remaining 2 cups water. Add the toasted spices, ginger, lemongrass, sugar, and sea salt. Simmer over low heat for 20 minutes, stirring occasionally. Then pass the soup through a fine-mesh sieve into a clean bowl, pressing on the contents with a spoon. Discard the solids and set the soup aside to cool. Then place it in the refrigerator to chill.

Whisk the yogurt in a bowl until smooth and stir it into the chilled mango soup. Ladle the soup into chilled bowls and garnish with the reserved mango slices and a scattering of pink peppercorns. Serve with the Sesame-Lime Cookies.

SESAME-LIME COOKIES   MAKES APPROXIMATELY 16 COOKIES

I have adapted this recipe from Deborah Madison's beautiful and informative cookbook *Local Flavors*. The crunchy texture with the hint of lime is a perfect accompaniment to the mango soup.

2 large egg whites

Pinch sea salt

1 tablespoon lime juice

⅔ cup sugar

½ teaspoon toasted sesame oil

⅓ cup all-purpose flour, sifted

½ teaspoon ground ginger

Grated zest of 1 lime

4 tablespoons (½ stick) butter, melted and cooled

½ cup sesame seeds, toasted

Preheat the oven to 375°F. Cover two baking sheets with parchment paper, or lightly butter and flour them.

Whisk the egg whites, salt, lime juice, and sugar together in a large mixing bowl until the mixture is thick, almost the consistency of glue, and glossy. Stir in the sesame oil, flour, ginger, and lime zest until well combined. Then stir in the melted butter and sesame seeds.

Place tablespoons of the batter on the prepared baking sheets, leaving a good 3 inches between them. Using the back of the spoon, spread each mound out to form a thin round. Bake for 6 to 8 minutes, or until lightly browned.

Let the cookies cool for 30 seconds, then run a spatula under them to release them. Drape the cookies over a rolling pin until they have set into a curved shape, 1 to 2 minutes. (If they harden too quickly to drape, return them to the oven for a couple of seconds to soften.)

Store the cookies in an airtight container so they don't soften.

GOOD CAESAR SALAD

If, like me, you are tired of experiencing Caesar salads made with ambiguous greens and bland, sweet dressings, then you might like to try this recipe. Start with finding good greens: Look for red romaine lettuce, baby gem, also known as butter lettuce, or baby cos, or the beautiful red-specked Castelfranco lettuce. Next is a good Caesar dressing. Grate a piece of Parmesan cheese rather than using pregrated. Don't shy away from the anchovies: it is these salty creatures that make the dressing taste so good. And finally, make your own croutons—it's easy and makes good use of stale bread. I like the addition of a softly boiled egg to enrich this salad. SERVES 4

CROUTONS

Large chunk stale bread, preferably
    ciabatta or country-style bread,
    crust removed

DRESSING

¼ clove garlic, green shoot removed

Sea salt and freshly ground black
    pepper

3 to 4 anchovy fillets

1 large egg yolk

½ teaspoon Dijon mustard

1½ tablespoons white wine vinegar

1 teaspoon lemon juice

¾ cup vegetable oil

½ cup extra virgin olive oil

3 tablespoons freshly grated
    Parmesan cheese

SALAD

4 large eggs

Sea salt and freshly ground black
    pepper

2 heads romaine lettuce, or similar,
    cut into quarters lengthwise

4 ounces Parmesan shavings (16
    pieces made with a vegetable
    peeler)

12 anchovy fillets

½ red onion, thinly sliced, optional

Preheat the oven to 375°F.

Prepare the croutons: Use your fingers to rip the bread into small pieces. Place them on a baking sheet and bake until crisp and golden brown, about 8 minutes. Remove from the oven and set aside to cool.

Prepare the dressing: Pound the garlic with a pinch of sea salt and pepper in a mortar and pestle until it has completely broken down. Add the anchovies, egg yolk, mustard, vinegar, and lemon juice, stirring until well combined. Continue to stir, trickling in the vegetable oil, followed by the olive oil, until emulsified. If the dressing thickens and becomes stiff, add a few drops of water. Stir in the grated Parmesan and taste for seasoning. Add more lemon juice or vinegar if you need to sharpen the flavor. The finished dressing should have the consistency of heavy cream. The dressing can be prepared up to a day ahead, covered and refrigerated. Bring it back to room temperature before serving. (Alternatively, you can make the dressing in a food processor.)

To make the salad, bring a saucepan of water to a boil. Carefully add the eggs and cook for 6 minutes. Drain, and cool the eggs under cold running water (this will prevent the yolks from turning gray). Peel the cooled eggs and cut them in half lengthwise. Season them with sea salt and pepper. The egg yolks should be slightly soft and oozing.

Place the wedges of salad greens in a mixing bowl and stir in ¼ cup of the dressing, evenly coating the leaves. Place the greens on serving plates, layering with the Parmesan shavings. Nestle the softly boiled eggs into the greens, and drape the anchovy fillets over the yolks. Scatter the croutons and red onion rings, if desired, over the top, and serve.

PERSIMMON, DATE, AND PECORINO SALAD

I love the combination of sweet and salty flavors and the soft, chewy, and firm textures in this salad.

When serving persimmons raw, choose ultra-ripe Fuyu persimmons. They are available in the latter half of autumn and into winter. Before purchasing, gently squeeze a persimmon just as you would when choosing a peach or nectarine; if the flesh doesn't give slightly, the fruit will be inedible.

There are numerous varieties of dates. I particularly like medjool dates, often known as toffee dates because of their deep red, sticky, rich flesh.

If you can find Spanish Marcona almonds, buy them. They have an intense flavor and an unusual squat shape.

Look for a mature pecorino cheese for this salad. Its salty, dry flavor marries perfectly with the sweet dates.

The greens are optional. A few sprigs of frisée or upland cress are perfect as a starter. If you're serving the salad after the main course, you might want to skip the greens. SERVES 4

DRESSING
¼ teaspoon Dijon mustard

1 tablespoon cider vinegar

1 tablespoon walnut oil

3 tablespoons extra virgin olive oil

Sea salt and freshly ground black
    pepper

½ cup whole almonds, blanched or
    skin on

3 ripe Fuyu persimmons, peeled and
    cut into thin rounds

12 medjool dates, halved and pitted

4 to 5 ounces pecorino shavings (12
    pieces made with a vegetable
    peeler)

Handful frisée or upland cress,
    optional

Preheat the oven to 375°F.

Prepare the dressing: Place the mustard in a bowl and blend with the cider vinegar. Whisk in the walnut and olive oils. Season with sea salt and pepper to taste. Set aside.

Toast the almonds on a baking sheet in the oven until golden brown, 8 to 10 minutes. Set aside to cool.

Arrange the persimmon slices, dates, almonds, pecorino shavings, and fr sée, if desired, attractively on a serving plate. Drizzle the dressing over the top and serve.

SQUID WITH CHILE-LIME BLACK BEAN SALAD

I like to use dried black beans imported from Spain for this recipe. Their creamy, earthy flavor works wonderfully in soaking up the spicy chile and lime juice. You could also use adzuki beans or black-eyed peas.   SERVES 4

SALAD

¾ cup dried black beans, soaked in cold water overnight

1 small onion

1 hot chile pepper, such as a Thai chile

3 cloves garlic: 2 cloves crushed, 1 clove minced

14 sprigs cilantro: 12 sprigs coarsely chopped, 2 sprigs left whole

Sea salt

2 tablespoons extra virgin olive oil

Grated zest and juice of 1 lime

1 small red onion, finely diced

DRESSING

½ teaspoon finely chopped hot chile pepper, such as a Thai chile

¼ teaspoon minced garlic

Grated zest and juice of 1 lime

2 teaspoons Asian fish sauce

1 teaspoon sugar

2 teaspoons toasted sesame oil

2 teaspoons soy sauce

2 tablespoons light olive oil

2 tablespoons coarsely chopped fresh cilantro

Sea salt

4 to 6 ounces Asian greens, such as pak choi or bok choi

¾ pound medium-size squid with tentacles, cleaned (see page 195)

Sea salt

½ tablespoon olive oil

Drain the beans and place them in a large saucepan (large enough for the beans to double in size during cooking). Add the onion, chile, crushed garlic, and cilantro sprigs. Cover with water and bring to a boil. Reduce the heat, skim off any foam that forms on the surface, and lower the heat. Simmer gently until the beans have started to soften, approximately 30 minutes. Add a generous pinch of sea salt and continue to simmer until the beans are meltingly tender, another 30 minutes (the time depends on the age of the beans).

Drain, and place the beans in a mixing bowl. Add the olive oil, lime zest and juice, red onions, minced garlic, and chopped cilantro. Taste, and add more salt if needed. Cover loosely with a kitchen towel or plastic wrap, and set aside.

Prepare a hot grill or grill pan. To prepare the dressing, place the chile, garlic, lime zest and juice, fish sauce, and sugar in a bowl. Whisk in the sesame oil, soy sauce, and olive oil. Stir in the cilantro. Taste and add sea salt if necessary.

Bring a medium saucepan of salted water to a boil and add the Asian greens. Cook until they just start to wilt but still hold their shape, approximately 2 minutes. Drain well and place the greens in a mixing bowl. Add 2 tablespoons of the dressing, toss well, and cover loosely with a kitchen towel. Set aside.

Cut the squid body open and lay it flat on a chopping board. Using a sharp knife, score the flesh in a crisscross pattern, being careful not to cut all the way through. If the squid pieces are large, cut them in half. Place the squid in a bowl, season with sea salt, and toss with the olive oil.

Place the squid on the grill. (If cooking the squid in a sauté pan, don't be tempted to overcrowd the pan as this will result in the squid stewing in its own juice, which will make it tough and chewy.) Cook for 1 to 2 minutes on each side, or until the squid turns opaque and starts to curl at the edges. Place the squid in a mixing bowl and toss with 1 tablespoon of the dressing.

Layer the black beans and pak choi on serving plates, and arrange the squid on top. Drizzle with the remaining dressing and serve.

PREPARING SQUID:

Cleaned squid is easy to find in the supermarket. However, it isn't difficult to do at home, although it is not for the fainthearted: Gently pull the head of the squid, with the tentacles attached, away from the body. (It's a good idea to wear an apron for this, as the squid juices from the innards may squirt.) Feel around the head of the squid, where the tentacles meet, for a small, hard ball. Using a sharp knife, cut across the flesh on the tentacle side of this ball. Discard the ink sac (the ball), unless you plan to use it in another recipe, and any of the innards that are attached.

Remove the outer layer of purple skin from the squid body with your fingers. It should pull off easily. Place a couple of fingers inside the body and feel for the quill, the squid's transparent spine. Grab hold of this and gently pull it out, along with the remaining innards. Wash the body and tentacles in cold water before using.

CITRUS FRUITS

I love the natural zing that explodes from citrus fruit. It adds such vibrancy to meat, fish, salads, and vegetables. After visiting Robin Lauriault's citrus grove in Florida, I came back eager to experiment with the many varieties and hybrids. Trying to remember and understand them all can be rather confusing, especially those that are difficult to find. One of these is the Amber Sweet orange—an orange, tangerine, and grapefruit hybrid. It looks like a grapefruit, but its flavor is incredibly sweet—not overly acidic—with slight spicy tones. However, at the citrus grove I was very sad to see them left to rot on the ground. Apparently they have become a liability; because of their uncommon name, people do not favor them. Other citrus varieties you are likely to come across are satsumas, clementines, and honey tangerines (which are all types of mandarin orange), kumquats and limequats, red and white grapefruits, pomelos, Meyer lemons, blood oranges, Seville oranges, and navel and Valencia oranges.

Feel free to experiment with the many varieties of citrus when making these salads. Enjoy balancing their sweet and bitter juices. And if you come across Amber Sweet orange, don't hesitate to grab one. You will not be disappointed!

Blood orange

Clementine

Grapefruit

    Duncan (seeded white)

    Marsh (seedless white)

    Ruby (seedless, deep flesh color, reddish peel)

    Thompson (seedless pink)

Key lime

Kumquat

Limequat

Meyer lemon

Navel orange

Pomelo

Satsuma orange

Seville orange

Sweet orange

Tangelo

Tangerine

Ugli

Valencia orange

GRAPEFRUIT, BLUE CHEESE, AND CELERY SALAD

I've tried this salad with different types of blue cheese and find that a sharp and salty blue, such as Harbourne Blue or Roquefort, is particularly good. Stilton also works very well. For a milder, creamier blue, try Fourme d'Ambert. SERVES 4

2 grapefruits

1 large egg yolk

2 teaspoons white wine vinegar

½ cup extra virgin olive oil

½ cup vegetable oil

5 ounces blue cheese

Sea salt and freshly ground black pepper

1 small red onion, thinly sliced

3 stalks celery, sliced diagonally

4 handfuls peppery salad greens, such as dandelion, endive, watercress

1 tablespoon snipped fresh chives (¼-inch pieces)

Handful bite-size toasted croutons (see page 191)

Using a paring knife, remove the peel and pith from the grapefruits. Holding one of the grapefruits in your hand over a large bowl, with the other hand carefully cut into the flesh alongside the membranes, prying the segments out as neatly as possible. The bowl is there to catch the segments and excess juice. Squeeze the remains of the grapefruit, extracting the remaining juices. Repeat with the other grapefruit. Set the bowl aside.

Place the egg yolk, 3 tablespoons of the reserved grapefruit juice, and the vinegar in a food processor and blend for 30 to 40 seconds. Slowly pour the oils into the processor while it is running. If the dressing becomes too thick, add an extra splash of grapefruit juice. At this point the dressing should resemble mayonnaise. Add 6 to 7 grapefruit segments and approximately 1 ounce of the blue cheese, and process until combined. Now stir in 1 to 2 tablespoons grapefruit juice, or enough to achieve a pouring consistency. Season with sea salt and pepper to taste. You will end up with about 2 cups of dressing. Place it in the refrigerator until needed.

Soak the red onions in the remaining grapefruit juice for approximately 15 minutes (this slightly pickles the onion).

When ready to serve, toss the celery with the salad greens in a bowl. Add sea salt and pepper to taste, and distribute among four plates. Drain the red onions and arrange them over the salad greens. Coarsely crumble the remaining blue cheese and scatter it over the salad. Tuck the remaining grapefruit segments into the greens, give them a generous drizzle of the dressing, and scatter the croutons on top. Serve immediately.

CONFIT DUCK, FENNEL, BLOOD ORANGE, AND WATERCRESS SALAD

Confit of duck is commonly found throughout France and is a specialty of the southwestern region. The duck legs are cooked in duck or goose fat, then packed tight and covered in the fat, thus preserving the meat. When they are cooked for this salad, the meat is meltingly tender and flavorful and the skin is crisp and salty. This is not a difficult recipe, but you will need to plan ahead because the duck is marinated for 3 to 4 days before being slowly braised in duck fat. It can then be stored for many months, improving its flavor and texture. Therefore it is a good idea to make more than you require and store it for future use.
Duck fat can be purchased in most good-quality supermarkets or butcher shops. SERVES 4

CONFIT

1½ tablespoons sea salt

16 black peppercorns, lightly crushed

4 bay leaves, crushed

1 tablespoon fennel seeds, coarsely crushed

8 sprigs thyme

6 cloves garlic

4 duck legs

About 9 cups duck fat

DRESSING

1 shallot, thinly sliced

Grated zest of 1 blood orange, plus 1 tablespoon juice

1 tablespoon red wine vinegar

⅛ teaspoon minced garlic

¼ teaspoon Dijon mustard

2 tablespoons extra virgin olive oil

1 tablespoon walnut oil

Sea salt and freshly ground black pepper

2 bulbs fennel

4 blood oranges

1 bunch watercress, trimmed

Sea salt and freshly ground black pepper

PREPARE THE CONFIT:

Mix the sea salt, peppercorns, bay leaves, fennel seeds, and 6 of the thyme sprigs in a bowl. Coarsely chop 4 of the garlic cloves and stir them into the mixture. Sprinkle one third of the sea salt mixture over the bottom of a small dish that is just large enough to hold two duck legs side by side. Place 2 duck legs, fat side down, in the dish. Sprinkle another third of the salt mixture over the duck legs. Then place the 2 remaining duck legs on top, fat side up. Scatter the remaining salt mixture over the top and press the duck legs firmly together with the palm of your hand. Cover with plastic wrap and place a heavy object, such as a food can, on top to press the duck legs. Refrigerate for 2 days.

Remove the dish from the refrigerator, take out the duck legs, and drain away any excess liquid in the dish. Place the duck legs back in the dish in the same manner as before, weight them down, and refrigerate for 2 more days.

Remove the duck legs from the dish, scrape off the excess marinade, and set them aside.

Coarsely chop the remaining 2 cloves garlic and put them in a saucepan that is large enough to hold the 4 duck legs side by side. Add the duck fat and the remaining 2 thyme sprigs, and melt the fat over low heat. Gently immerse the duck legs in the melted fat and bring to a very low simmer. Cook, stirring them every so often, until they are tender, approximately 2 hours. While they are cooking, make sure they are always fully immersed in the fat, which must not exceed a slow simmer. When a skewer inserted into a duck leg moves the meat easily, they are ready.

PREPARE THE DRESSING:

Combine the shallots, blood orange zest and juice, vinegar, and garlic in a small bowl, and set aside to macerate for 15 minutes. Then whisk in the mustard, olive oil, and walnut oil. Season with sea salt and pepper to taste. Set aside.

FINISH THE SALAD:

Remove the fronds from the fennel bulbs and coarsely chop them. Add the chopped fronds to the dressing. Remove the outer layer of the fennel bulbs and wash the fennel hearts under cold running water. Slice them into thin rounds, avoiding the dense root at the base, and set aside.

Remove the peel and pith from the blood oranges, and slice them into 1/4-inch-thick rounds. Set aside.

Carefully remove the duck legs from the fat and place them, skin side down, in a sauté pan over low heat. Once the excess fat has melted, raise the heat and cook until the skin is crisp and golden brown, approximately 10 minutes in all. Turn the duck legs over and cook for another 5 minutes on the other side. Remove the duck legs from the pan and set aside.

While the duck legs are crisping, place the watercress, fennel, and oranges in a bowl, and season with a pinch of sea salt and pepper. Add a large spoonful of the dressing and toss gently, being careful not to break the orange slices. Divide this among four plates. Place a duck leg on each plate and finish with a drizzle of the remaining dressing. Serve immediately.

CITRUS AND ENDIVE SALAD
WITH MINT YOGURT

I suggest using a variety of citrus fruit for this easy, refreshing salad, but don't think it's limited to just this selection. Make substitutions, or make it with just one type—it'll still be delicious. SERVES 4 TO 6

⅓ cup whole blanched almonds

5 tablespoons thick Greek yogurt, strained in a coffee filter for 10 minutes (see Note, page 97)

5 tablespoons grapefruit juice

Small pinch sea salt

Smidgeon minced garlic

2 tablespoons coarsely chopped fresh mint

1 pink grapefruit, skin and pith removed

1 white grapefruit, skin and pith removed

2 blood oranges, skin and pith removed

1 honey tangerine, skin and pith removed

3 heads chicory or belgian endive, leaves separated

Preheat the oven to 375°F.

Place the almonds on a baking sheet and toast in the oven until golden brown, about 10 minutes. Remove them from the oven and allow to cool.

Mix the yogurt, grapefruit juice, sea salt, garlic, and mint together in a bowl. Set it aside.

Cut all the citrus fruit into rounds or segments, whichever you like. (I tend to do a mixture of both, as it looks more interesting.)

Place the endive leaves in a salad bowl and stir in the yogurt dressing. Arrange the endive and citrus fruit attractively on a serving platter, and finish with a scattering of toasted almonds.

SHRIMP, ROASTED CHERRY TOMATO, AND WATERCRESS SALAD

This is perhaps the only time I use a fresh tomato in the winter. Cherry tomatoes add a great acidity to this salad and when roasted, their natural sugars become more pronounced.

Piquillo peppers are sold in fine supermarkets and delicatessens. They are wood-roasted and hand-peeled before being canned in olive oil. They have a really wonderful smoky flavor, with a gentle heat. SERVES 4 AS AN APPETIZER OR 2 AS A MAIN COURSE

DRESSING

Grated zest and juice of 1 lemon

Grated zest and juice of 1 lime

½ teaspoon finely chopped chile pepper, such as a Thai chile

½ teaspoon minced garlic

3 tablespoons extra virgin olive oil

Pinch sea salt

9 cups Vegetable Stock (page 225) or water

16 large shrimp in their shells

1 pound cherry tomatoes

1 tablespoon extra virgin olive oil

1 clove garlic, thinly sliced

2 tablespoons fresh rosemary leaves

Sea salt and freshly ground black pepper

Generous handful watercress, trimmed

4 scallions, sliced diagonally

3 piquillo peppers, sliced into strips

⅓ cup fresh cilantro leaves

Prepare the dressing: Place the lemon zest and juice, lime zest and juice, chile, and garlic in a bowl. Whisk in the olive oil and season with a pinch of sea salt. Set aside.

Preheat the oven to 400°F.

Bring the vegetable stock to a boil in a large saucepan. Add the shrimp and cook until they turn a deep pink, 1 to 2 minutes. Drain and spread the shrimp cut on a baking sheet to cool. Once they are cool enough to handle, peel off the shells and use a paring knife to remove the dark vein that runs across the top of the shrimp. (Do not be tempted to run the shrimp under water, as this will eliminate some of their flavor.)

Place the peeled shrimp in a bowl and toss with 1 tablespoon of the dressing. Set aside to marinate.

Place the cherry tomatoes in an ovenproof dish, drizzle with the olive oil, and scatter the sliced garlic and rosemary leaves over the top. Season to taste with sea salt and pepper. Roast for approximately 15 minutes, or until the tomatoes start to brown. Remove them from the oven and allow to cool to room temperature.

When ready to serve, gently toss the watercress in a bowl with the scallions, piquillo peppers, and cilantro leaves. Arrange this on individual plates, and tuck the shrimp and roasted tomatoes into the salad. Drizzle with the remaining dressing and serve.

Try making this with lobster or crabmeat as well. I like to serve potato chips on the side. SERVES 2

8 cups Vegetable Stock (page 225)
   or water

8 shrimp in their shells

3 tablespoons Mayonnaise (page 223)

1 teaspoon tomato paste

1 teaspoon ketchup

Tabasco sauce, to taste

1½ teaspoons prepared horseradish

Sea salt and freshly ground black
   pepper

RELISH

¼ teaspoon finely chopped hot chile
   pepper, such as a Thai chile

½ cup drained and coarsely chopped
   canned tomatoes

1 tablespoon tomato paste

1 tablespoon red wine vinegar

1 tablespoon prepared horseradish

Smidgeon minced garlic

Grated zest of 1 lemon

Sea salt and freshly ground black
   pepper to taste

2 scallions, thinly sliced

¼ cucumber, peeled, halved, seeded,
   and thinly sliced

2 rolls

4 leaves romaine lettuce

Bring the vegetable stock to a boil in a large saucepan. Add the shrimp and cook until they turn pink, 1 to 2 minutes. Be careful not to overcook the shrimp, or they will be tough and rubbery. Drain the shrimp and spread them out on a baking sheet to cool. Once they are cool enough to handle, peel off the shells and use a paring knife to remove the dark vein that runs across the top of the shrimp. (Do not be tempted to run the shrimp under water, as this will eliminate some of their flavor.) Cover and refrigerate until ready to use.

Place the mayonnaise in a bowl and add the tomato paste, ketchup, a splash of Tabasco, and the grated horseradish. Taste and adjust the seasoning with sea salt and pepper. Refrigerate until ready to use.

Prepare the relish: Combine all the relish ingredients in a bowl, mix well, and refrigerate until ready to serve.

In a large bowl, combine the shrimp, scallions, and cucumbers with the mayonnaise mixture. When you are ready to serve, cut the rolls in half horizontally and divide the romaine leaves between them. Scoop the shrimp salad onto the rolls. Serve with the Tomato Cocktail Relish on the side.

SMOKED SALMON CLUB

Try making these as bite-size hors d'oeuvres served with pink champagne!   MAKES 2 SANDWICHES

2 tablespoons crème fraîche

1 tablespoon finely snipped fresh chives

½ teaspoon grated lemon zest

Sea salt and freshly ground black pepper

6 slices bread, such as potato-dill, whole-grain, or pumpernickel

¼ cucumber, peeled, halved, seeded, and thinly sliced

4 ounces smoked salmon, thinly sliced

Small handful watercress or upland cress, trimmed

Place the crème fraîche in a bowl and stir in the chives, lemon zest, and sea salt and pepper to taste.

Toast the bread.

Place a small spoonful of the chive crème fraîche on 1 slice of toast. Layer one fourth of the cucumbers, smoked salmon, and watercress on top, then sandwich with a second piece of toast. Repeat the layers, finishing with a third piece of toast on top. Press down firmly and secure the sandwich with toothpicks. Repeat the process for the second sandwich. Cut the sandwiches in half diagonally, arrange on plates, and serve.

SPICY STEAK SANDWICH WITH CHIPOTLE MAYONNAISE AND BUTTERMILK FRIED ONION RINGS

I love rummaging through my spice cupboard to prepare a marinade for steak. I am not so sure that I can ever repeat a marinade, but that is half the fun. Using this recipe as a guide, experiment at making your own. Cumin and coriander are great spices to blend for a steak. I love the wonderfully smoky Turkish pepper called urfa-biber rubbed into a steak. It has a deep dried-fruit aroma with just the right amount of heat.

You can marinate the steak and prepare the Chipotle Mayonnaise a day ahead.   SERVES 2

STEAK

1 clove garlic

¼ teaspoon sea salt

½ teaspoon ground ancho chile

½ teaspoon ground chipotle chile

Pinch cayenne pepper

¼ teaspoon dried oregano

1 tablespoon lemon or lime juice

1 tablespoon extra virgin olive oil

Two 6-ounce steaks (skirt, strip loin, ribeye, or filet)

CHIPOTLE MAYONNAISE

1 teaspoon cumin seeds, toasted and ground

¼ teaspoon ground chipotle chile

6 tablespoons Aioli (page 24)

BUTTERMILK ONION RINGS

1 large white onion, sliced ¼ inch thick

1 cup buttermilk

8 cups vegetable oil for deep-frying

⅔ cup all-purpose flour

½ cup coarsely ground yellow cornmeal

1 tablespoon fresh thyme leaves

¾ teaspoon sea salt

Prepare the steaks: Place the garlic clove and sea salt in a mortar and pestle and crush to a paste. Stir in the ancho chile, chipotle chile, cayenne, dried oregano, lemon juice, and olive oil. (Alternatively, process all these ingredients together in a food processor.)

Place the steaks on a plate and smear the marinade all over them. Cover loosely with plastic wrap and store in the refrigerator. Approximately 30 minutes before you are ready to cook them, remove the steaks from the refrigerator and allow them to return to room temperature.

Prepare the mayonnaise: Combine the cumin, chipotle chile, and aioli in a small bowl. Mix well, cover, and refrigerate until needed.

Prepare the onion rings: Separate the rings of the onion and place them in a bowl. Add the buttermilk and set aside for approximately 30 minutes.

While the onions are soaking, heat the vegetable oil in a deep, heavy saucepan to 375°F. Combine the flour, cornmeal, thyme, sea salt, and pepper on a rimmed plate, and mix well. Set it aside.

While the onions are still soaking, cook the steaks: Heat a sauté pan over high heat. Add the olive oil and butter. Place the steaks in the pan and brown on both sides until they are crisp on the outside and pink in the middle, 2 to 3 minutes per side. While they are cooking, squeeze the lime juice over the steaks (the fat may spit, so be careful). Using a large spoon, continually baste the steaks with the lime juice, butter, and olive oil. If you prefer your steak cooked further, cook it for a few more minutes. Remove the steaks from the heat and let them rest while you fry the onions.

Remove the onion rings, one by one, from the buttermilk and dip them into the flour mixture. Slowly place a few onion rings in the hot oil and cook, stirring every so often, for 3 to 4 minutes, or until golden brown. Remove the rings from the pan with a slotted spoon and place them on paper towels to drain. Repeat with the remaining onion rings. Season the rings liberally with salt and pepper. If you need to keep them warm, pop them into the oven for a minute or two.

½ teaspoon freshly ground black pepper

1 tablespoon olive oil

1 tablespoon butter

Juice of 1 lime

4 slices bread such as onion bread, ciabatta, sourdough, or rye

Small handful salad greens, such as arugula, romaine, or watercress

To assemble the sandwiches, spread the mayonnaise on 2 of the slices of bread. Divide the salad greens between them. Place a steak on top of each one and sandwich with the remaining bread. Serve the hot onion rings on the side.

AVOCADO, FENNEL, AND PARMESAN SALAD
WITH LIME DRESSING   SERVES 2 TO 4

This is a very clean-tasting salad that will refresh the palate after eating the steak sandwich.

1 bulb fennel, tough outer layer removed
1 stalk celery
1 avocado
Handful arugula leaves
1 head belgian endive, leaves separated
2 to 3 ounces Parmesan shavings (8 to 12 pieces made with a vegetable peeler)
Handful croutons (page 191)
Sea salt and freshly ground black pepper
1 tablespoon lime juice
1 tablespoon white balsamic vinegar or white wine vinegar
3 tablespoons extra virgin olive oil

Using a sharp knife or a mandoline, shave the fennel. Place the shavings in a bath of cold water. Using a vegetable peeler, shave the celery lengthwise into long strips; add them to the cold water. (The water will keep the vegetables crisp.)

Peel the avocado and cut the flesh into long strips.

Place the arugula and endive in a large bowl. Drain the fennel and celery, pat them dry, and add them to the bowl along with the avocado, Parmesan shavings, and croutons. Season with salt and pepper to taste. Add the lime juice, vinegar, and olive oil, and toss well. Taste and adjust the seasonings if necessary. Serve immediately.

PEPPERS

Adding one or more of a variety of peppers can alter the spice mix dramatically. You can use fresh chile peppers, dried chili peppers, and/or smoked chile peppers, and then there are also umpteen varieties of peppercorns to choose from, all offering individual and often complex flavors.

Don't be shy about blending spices; it's hard to go really wrong. Follow a few recipes first, then start to experiment. Spices, and especially peppers, are great to have on hand to jazz up a simple meal of steamed or grilled meat or fish.

HAM AND BRIE SANDWICH WITH APPLE-WALNUT SALAD

So, how do we turn this standard deli sandwich into something worth eating?

First of all, buy good-quality ham. There are many types to choose from. Start by looking for a ham without added water. The next thing to look for is a ham that has been cooked on the bone. Prosciutto cotto, speck, and applewood-smoked hams are all good.

I prefer to cook the ham myself. To do this buy a piece of gammon (pork which has been soaked in brine) and simmer it in vegetable stock for 25 minutes per pound. Then remove it from the cooking liquor and brush the skin with a glaze of honey, brown sugar, and orange juice. Place it into a preheated 375°F oven for approximately 20 minutes until the outside of the ham is glazed, shining, and golden brown.

This recipe calls for making your own mustard. It's very easy to do and never fails to impress. Just plan on soaking the mustard seeds a day ahead. MAKES 2 SANDWICHES

MUSTARD

1 cup mustard seeds

3 cups water

5 teaspoons sea salt

Pinch freshly ground white pepper

1 cup white wine vinegar

3 to 4 tablespoons coarsely chopped fresh tarragon

1 tablespoon horseradish, prepared or freshly grated

2 slices whole-grain or pumpernickel bread

½ ounce watercress, trimmed

¼ pound sliced baked or smoked ham (see headnote)

¼ pound Brie cheese

1 stalk celery

Small handful celery leaves

1 apple, such as McIntosh, Braeburn, or Granny Smith, quartered and cored

6 walnut halves, toasted

1 tablespoon walnut oil

Sea salt and freshly ground black pepper

Prepare the mustard: Combine the mustard seeds and water in a large bowl, stir well, and refrigerate overnight.

Drain the mustard seeds and add the sea salt, white pepper, and vinegar. Coarsely puree in a blender in batches. Transfer the mustard to a bowl and stir in the tarragon and horseradish until well combined. Spoon into a clean storage jar and refrigerate. It will keep well for at least 6 months.

To make the sandwiches, spread a thin layer of the mustard on each slice of bread. Divide the watercress between them. Arrange the ham and Brie on top.

Slice the celery diagonally and combine with the celery leaves in a bowl. Cut the apple into thin wedges and add them to the celery. Add the walnuts and walnut oil, season with a pinch of sea salt and pepper, and toss together.

Arrange the sandwiches on two plates, with the apple salad alongside.

TURKEY SANDWICH WITH CRANBERRY-PEAR RELISH

The Cranberry-Pear Relish turns a familiar sandwich into something really scrumptious. Choose good-quality bread as well. I like the crunchy texture and flavor of walnut bread. A pecan bread would also work well. MAKES 2 SANDWICHES

4 slices walnut bread

2 tablespoons Cranberry-Pear Relish (see below)

Small handful salad greens

4 slices bacon, cooked crisp

¼ pound sliced roasted turkey

Sea salt and freshly ground black pepper

Place 2 slices of the bread on a cutting board and spread the relish over them. Divide the salad greens between the 2 slices, and arrange the bacon and turkey on top. Season with sea salt and pepper to taste. Place the remaining slices of walnut bread on top, press down, and cut in half

CRANBERRY-PEAR RELISH

If you are having roasted turkey during the holiday season, it is definitely worth making a large jar of this relish to accompany the meat. Note that the pears and cranberries need to marinate overnight.

1½ pounds pears, such as Comice, Bartlett, or Conference, peeled, quartered, and cored

6 ounces cranberries

3 tablespoons light brown sugar

Grated zest of 1 orange

Juice of 2 oranges

½ teaspoon sea salt

One 2-inch cinnamon stick

2 whole cloves

Slice the quartered pears into thin wedges and place them, with the cranberries, in a bowl. Add the brown sugar, orange zest and juice, and salt, and stir. Tie the cinnamon stick and cloves in a cheesecloth bundle and add it to the bowl. Cover the bowl with plastic wrap and refrigerate overnight or for at least 12 hours.

When you are ready to cook the relish, preheat the oven to 375°F.

Transfer the relish to a saucepan and bring it to a boil over medium heat. Reduce the heat and simmer, stirring every so often, for approximately 30 minutes, or until the pears are tender and the liquid has reduced to a jamlike consistency. Discard the cheesecloth bundle.

Bring a saucepan of water to a boil, and submerge a metal spoon and the lid of a 2-pint canning jar in the water for 5 minutes to sterilize them. At the same time, heat the meticulously clean canning jar in the oven for 10 minutes. Then, using the sterilized spoon, place the relish in the jar and seal it with the sterilized lid. This will keep for 3 months. (If you are going to consume the relish within 2 to 3 weeks, you do not need to sterilize the jar first. Just keep the relish refrigerated.)

PAIN PERDU WITH ROASTED APPLES

Pain perdu means lost, or stale, bread in French. The bread is soaked in milk, dipped in egg, and then panfried in butter until golden. It is otherwise known as French toast—created as a heavenly way of using up a day-old baguette. I like to use a sweet-tasting or butter-enriched bread such as brioche or challah.   SERVES 4

ROASTED APPLES

2 apples, such as Braeburn, McIntosh, or Granny Smith, peeled, quartered, and cored

¼ teaspoon ground cinnamon

Pinch ground nutmeg

Grated zest of 1 lemon

4 tablespoons (½ stick) butter

¼ cup light brown sugar

PAIN PERDU

2 cups heavy cream

1 vanilla bean

¼ cup confectioners' sugar

4 large eggs, beaten

4 thick slices brioche or challah

4 to 6 tablespoons clarified butter (see Note)

Combine the apples, cinnamon, nutmeg, and lemon zest in a bowl, and toss to mix. Set aside for 20 minutes or so.

Melt the butter in a sauté pan over medium heat. Add the apples and sauté gently until lightly colored, approximately 10 minutes. Sprinkle the brown sugar over the apples, and keeping the pan on the heat, toss the apples until the butter and sugar have begun to combine and caramelize. Then, stirring intermittently, let the apples cook until they are soft but still holding their shape, about 5 minutes. Remove the pan from the heat and keep warm.

To prepare the pain perdu, pour the heavy cream into a saucepan. Split the vanilla bean in half lengthwise and scrape the seeds into the cream. Add the empty bean as well. Over low heat, stir the confectioners' sugar into the cream until dissolved. Remove the pan from the heat and allow the cream and vanilla to infuse for 15 minutes. Remove the vanilla bean and set the cream aside to cool.

Combine the eggs with the cooled cream. Soak the bread in this mixture for a generous 10 minutes.

Preheat the oven 325°F. Warm the clarified butter in a large sauté pan over medium heat. When the butter is just starting to sizzle, remove 1 slice of bread from the cream mixture, squeeze it gently, and add it to the pan. Cook until the bread is golden brown on the bottom; then flip it over and cook on the other side, about 8 minutes in all. Transfer the bread to a plate and keep it warm in the oven. Repeat with the remaining 3 slices of bread.

Serve immediately, with the roasted apples spooned over the bread. If the caramel sauce surrounding the apples has cooled, it may be too hard to spoon over the pain perdu. Add a splash of water to the sauté pan and return it to the heat for a couple of minutes, stirring well to soften.

NOTE:
To clarify butter, place some butter in a bowl over a saucepan of simmering water. The clear fat will slowly separate to the top. With a ladle or spoon, carefully remove the fat, leaving the white solids in the bowl to be discarded. Clarified butter stands up to higher temperatures and is often used for frying.

BASIC RECIPES

FLAT BREAD

This yeast-based bread can be used for sandwiches, pizza, or as a side to accompany other dishes. The basic recipe can be flavored with anything from herbs and spices to roasted or grilled vegetables and cheese. Try this bread for the lamb sandwich on page 42 or the Moroccan chicken sandwich on page 101. MAKES 8 BREADS

1 ounce fresh yeast

½ tablespoon sugar

1 cup warm water

1 cup all-purpose flour

2⅔ cups bread flour

1½ tablespoons sea salt, plus extra for seasoning the surface

½ cup extra virgin olive oil, plus extra for drizzling

Mix the yeast with the sugar and warm water in a large bowl. Allow to rest for about 5 minutes, or until the mixture starts to bubble.

Add both flours to the yeast mixture, and stir in the salt and olive oil. Place this in the bowl of a standing mixer. Using the dough hook, knead the dough for 8 to 12 minutes, or until it is smooth and slightly sticky.

Coat a large, clean bowl with olive oil and add the dough, turning to coat it in the oil. Cover the bowl with a kitchen towel and leave it in a warm place for approximately 2 hours, or until the dough has doubled in size.

Meanwhile, preheat the oven to 450°F. Place two baking sheets in the oven to preheat.

Transfer the dough to a lightly floured surface. (If you are making the flat bread on page 101, add the coriander seeds now.) Knead it for 1 to 2 minutes, until it is smooth. Divide the dough into golf-ball-size pieces and let them rest for 10 minutes.

Roll out each ball on a lightly floured surface to form a round approximately 8 inches in diameter. Place 2 rounds on the preheated baking sheets, drizzle with extra virgin olive oil, and sprinkle with sea salt. Bake until golden brown and crisp, 6 to 8 minutes. Remove the flat breads and place them on a cooling rack. Repeat with the remaining dough.

Store the breads in an airtight container for up to 2 days.

PASTRY TART SHELL

MAKES ONE 10-INCH TART SHELL

1½ cups all-purpose flour

¼ teaspoon sea salt

8 tablespoons (1 stick) butter, cut into thin pieces

3 tablespoons beaten egg

1 tablespoon cold water

Preheat the oven to 375°F.

Sift the flour and sea salt into a large mixing bowl. Rub the butter into the flour until it resembles coarse meal. Add the egg and water and stir until it forms a dough. On a lightly floured surface, knead the dough gently until smooth, about 20 seconds.

Wrap the dough in plastic and let it rest in the refrigerator for at least 30 minutes or as long as 5 days.

When ready to use, allow the dough to come to room temperature. On a lightly floured surface, roll the dough out to form a large round, approximately ¼ inch thick. Line a 10-inch tart shell with the dough, pressing it evenly over the base and sides. Refrigerate for 30 minutes before baking (to prevent shrinkage).

To prebake the shell, line it with parchment paper and fill the shell with dried beans. Place in the oven and bake for 10 minutes. Remove the parchment and beans, then bake for 8 minutes more, or until the pastry is crisp and golden brown. Cool and remove from the pan. The tart shell will keep for 1 day stored in an airtight container, or it can be frozen.

MAYONNAISE

1 large egg yolk

Sea salt and freshly ground black pepper to taste

½ teaspoon Dijon mustard

½ teaspoon white wine vinegar

½ cup extra virgin olive oil

6 tablespoons sunflower oil or grapeseed oil

1 to 2 teaspoons lemon juice

Mix the egg yolk, sea salt and pepper, mustard, and white wine vinegar in a bowl until thick and gluey. Then slowly drizzle the olive oil, and then the sunflower oil, into the mixture, drop by drop, vigorously beating until emulsified. If it becomes too thick, add a drop of the lemon juice and then continue to beat until all the oil has been added. Adjust the seasoning and consistency with more sea salt, pepper, or lemon juice as needed. (You can also make the mayonnaise in a food processor, using the same method.)

The mayonnaise will keep, covered and refrigerated, for up to 2 days.

BEER BATTER

2 cups all-purpose flour

Sea salt to taste

1 bottle (12 fluid ounces) beer, at room temperature

Mix the flour and sea salt together in a medium-size bowl. Whisk in the beer until combined with the flour to form a batter. Use immediately

VEGETABLE STOCK

Use this recipe as a basic guide, utilizing the vegetables you have available. MAKES APPROXIMATELY 2 QUARTS

9 cups water

4 carrots, coarsely chopped

4 stalks celery, coarsely chopped

2 onions, coarsely chopped

1 leek (white part only), coarsely
  sliced

3 cloves garlic, crushed

Good pinch sea salt

4 black peppercorns, crushed

Small handful parsley stems

Small handful rosemary stems

Small handful thyme stems

2 bay leaves

Put all the ingredients into a large pot and place it over high heat. Bring to a boil and skim off any scum that forms on the surface. Lower the heat and simmer for approximately 25 minutes.

Strain the stock into a bowl, discarding the solids. Allow to cool, then refrigerate or freeze. The stock will remain fresh-tasting for about 2 days in the refrigerator. Freeze it if you intend to store it for longer than 5 days.

BIBLIOGRAPHY

Davidson, Alan. *The Oxford Companion to Food*. New York: Oxford University Press, 1999.

Ellis, Hattie. *Eating England*. London: Mitchell Beazley, 2001.

Henry, Diana. *Crazy Water, Pickled Lemons*. London: Mitchell Beazley, 2002.

Madison, Deborah. *Local Flavors*. New York: Broadway Books, 2002.

Norris, Lucy. *Pickled*. New York: Stewart, Tabori and Chang, 2003.

Vaughan, J. G., and C. A. Geissler, et al. *The New Oxford Book of Food Plants*. New York: Oxford University Press, 1997.

Waters, Alice. *Chez Panisse Menu Cookbook*. New York: Random House, 1982.

INDEX

sandwiches of, see sandwich(es),
    winter
seasonal items of, 173
soups of, see soup(s), winter

yogurt:
    dressing, with swordfish, spicy red
        lentil and zucchini salad, 84–85
    Greek, with rhubarb-strawberry
        puree, 23
    mint, with citrus and endive salad,
        203
    thick, with vanilla-poached rhubarb
        on raisin-nut bread, 45

zest, 107
    orange, 67
zucchini, 61
    swordfish, spicy red lentil salad with
        yogurt dressing, 84–85